THE ART OF WINNING

THE ART OF WINNING

Dennis Conner

with Edward Claflin

Foreword by Donald Trump

ST. MARTIN'S PRESS / NEW YORK

Design by Claudia Carlson

Library of Congress Cataloging-in-Publication Data

Conner, Dennis.
    The art of winning.

    1. Teamwork (Sports)   2. Success.   3. Motivation
(Psychology)   I. Claflin, Edward.   II. Title.
GV706.8.C66   1989   796'.01   88-29850
ISBN 0-312-02543-2

First Edition
10 9 8 7 6 5 4 3 2 1

To my family, friends, and teammates
who have helped me along the way.

Contents

Foreword

It would be hard to pick two people whose backgrounds are more different than Dennis Conner's and mine. I'm East Coast; he's West. While I was growing up in New York and learning the real estate business, Dennis was sailing the waters off San Diego and becoming a super-competitive racer. While I was building Trump Tower, Dennis was preparing his defense of the America's Cup in Newport; while I was designing Trump's Hotel and Casino in Atlantic City, Dennis was plotting his strategy to recapture the America's Cup from the Australians.

Given all these differences, it's remarkable how much we have in common. Maybe it's because we both understand the meaning of tunnel vision: once we've decided to do something, we go for it with everything we've got. Dennis calls it "the commitment to the commitment." I call it "thinking big." It means setting your sights on a goal that may seem unattainable, and achieving it.

There are some other areas where Dennis and I also see eye to eye. Working with people, for instance. It doesn't pay to work with the second best—people who *almost* know what they're talking about, or people who can't meet deadlines, stand up under pressure, or get the job done. You need the *best.* For me, that means the best architects, the best developers, the best builders and interior designers. For Dennis, that means the best sail and yacht designers, the best shore team, the best tactician, navigator, and crew.

Then there's the attention to detail. Dennis ties it into his "no-excuse-to-lose" principle. If there's anything that can be done better, more efficiently, you try to do it that way—because a single missed detail could turn into your Achilles' heel.

But beyond the commitment, the determination to find the best people, and the attention to detail, Dennis symbolizes the strongest positive attitude. He has the drive that creates winners. And his championship attitude pervades every page of this book.

I'll never forget my first encounter with Dennis Conner. It was in the early days of the campaign to win the 1987 America's Cup, when Dennis had to find corporate sponsors to get the funding he needed to build *Stars & Stripes*. With his syndicate committed to spending millions of dollars to build a winning 12-meter, there was no one better able to raise the money than Dennis himself.

Like everything else he takes on, Dennis threw one thousand percent of his effort into getting those sponsorships.

On the day it was my turn for Dennis's visit, he came uninvited and sat in the lobby outside my office. My secretaries have the thankless duty of discouraging unexpected visitors, and they did their best. Dennis wouldn't go away. The secretaries tried to be polite, but Dennis gave them two choices: either they could let him see me, or they could call the police.

I was prepared to give him just a few minutes of my time, but when he came into my office and started to talk about his plans for winning the Cup from the Australians in '87, I listened with growing interest. He had the promotion all planned, down to the last detail, and he could tell me exactly where the Trump organization would fit into his plans if we decided to go for it.

It was all very low-key, the Dennis Conner style—no fireworks or fist-pounding. But I was impressed. Even though I wasn't interested in the specific promotional program that Dennis had designed for me, I was fascinated with the guy who was putting together a campaign that had thousands of different working parts. I began to see just how complex that campaign actually was. All of the parts *had* to work right—from conceptualizing new designs to engineering new boats, from stitching sails to providing fresh sandwiches for the crew, from multimillion-dollar fundraising to having the right number of spare shackles on a tender.

Later I did commit to the campaign, and I underwrote the ticker-tape parade up Fifth Avenue in New York City after the race. I didn't help just because Dennis Conner made a great sales pitch. I was there because you meet guys like this just a few times in your life, and when you do, you want to be on their side.

Now that I've watched Dennis Conner for a few years and seen him at work, the other thing that I've recognized about him is that he has a "Dennis Conner Method"—a unique way of tackling problems, dealing with people, and getting things done. The people who work with Dennis get to know that method, and it's part of what makes it possible for him to build great teams and keep his businesses well managed and running smoothly. Having a consistent approach to problem-solving, team-building, and deal-making makes for a consistent style of management. And I think that's one of the most important elements of leadership.

Dennis Conner is best known for his America's Cup victories. But he has also achieved hard-earned success as an entrepreneur and business leader. What's interesting is how the Dennis Conner Method applies to whatever enterprise he's involved in. Whether he's building a campaign for the next America's Cup, managing one of his current businesses, or launching a new venture, Dennis Conner inspires great teamwork. And he commands tremendous loyalty. But even with the most loyal team, it takes extraordinary management skills to run several businesses *and* put in hundreds of hours of sailing practice every year.

What makes it all happen is a method that involves all the elements of winning that he describes in his book. In the past, people could only learn the Dennis Conner Method by *doing,* by working with him. Until he wrote this book, he had never sat down and explained the secrets to anyone, not to his crew nor to his closest associates. But it's a method that produces great results. The people with Dennis Conner make the commitment that it takes to win big; they are outstanding, competitive performers; and they share the fire that comes with a great competitive spirit.

The Art of Winning describes a method that consistently produces results, whether you're designing and racing the fastest sailboat in the world or constructing the most spectacular casino on the boardwalk. You can use the strategies in this book to succeed in your job, to win in a sport, to focus your activities at home or at work, to inspire other people, or to turn a sideline avocation into a big win with a lot of personal satisfaction. This book tells about ideals—setting personal goals and dreaming your dream—but it also has highly practical tips on competitive strategy. And it has some of the best ideas on motivating people and building a team that I've read.

For the people who have asked me, "What's Dennis Conner's secret? How does he keep going like that—and winning?" the answer is here. This is his method, and I think it will work for everyone.

The day I rode on the float in the ticker-tape parade that welcomed Dennis and his crew back home in '87, the outpouring of enthusiasm from a crowd of half a million New Yorkers was overwhelming. And when Dennis successfully defended the Cup in 1988 against an unexpected, unorthodox challenge from New Zealand, there was another outburst of celebration. Coming back from the defeat of '83, Dennis appreciated the importance of both races. But what I remember personally was that day in 1987 when the faces in the cheering crowd told me Dennis Conner had won a triumph for millions of Americans who took pride in the determination and accomplishments of the whole team of *Stars & Stripes.*

Everyone identifies with a winner. Who wouldn't like to be a success? We all want to achieve our real potential in whatever we do. It's up to you, of course, to decide on your goal and make the commitment to reach it. But *The Art of Winning* reveals Dennis Conner's unique, best-kept secrets for getting there—and that's enough to give everyone a big head start.

Donald Trump
New York

Introduction

Here's what it's like:

You wake up every morning knowing that you must accomplish more than can possibly be done in the next twenty-four hours— more than you have ever done any other day of your life. You are eager to begin and reluctant to close your eyes at the day's end. You keep thinking of details you might have overlooked. You try to outguess and outmaneuver the competition. You don't want them to know your plans, but you want to know every detail of theirs. You practice, and practice some more—always looking for a better way, always pushing at the limits of the possible. You don't want to waste a single moment that you *could* be devoting to the effort. If you ever have a moment to relax, you think about what you could be doing instead of relaxing.

By the day of the first race, you know you have done everything you possibly can to prepare. You wish you had another day, another hour, another minute, but time has run out. You have taken away every possible excuse to lose. You have the best boat, the best sails, the best equipment, the best team that can be formed in the time you've had—and now there's nothing you can do but integrate all these elements and sail the race.

Afterward comes the moment of victory. It's payday! The bells and whistles from the spectator fleet fill your ears. All the hard work and all the sacrifices have come to this, the sweetest moment of all, the moment of winning.

The Challenge of Winning

In the many months since the *Stars & Stripes* team and I brought the America's Cup back home in 1987, I have reflected on the three and a half years of preparation that led to triumph in Freemantle. I've written two books about the victory, delivered over one hundred talks, and been fortunate to receive a number of awards and honorary degrees. All this was a direct result of those long days, short nights, and hours of preparation.

Meanwhile, there are other challenges. For years I have had a great partnership with which to invest in real estate opportunities, and have owned and run Dennis Conner Interiors, a carpet and drapery company with $4,000,000 in annual sales. Since the '87 America's Cup, I have started a third business, Dennis Conner Sports, to market sailing and other sports-related enterprises. Preparation continues for the next America's Cup race—and the one after—with all the activities that go into each one of these multimillion-dollar campaigns. In addition, there are opportunities and exciting new enterprises that come within reach every day.

Many good things have come out of that winning experience. And because I'm often asked to talk about it, I've had to think about aspects of winning that have interested me ever since I started racing sailboats, elements of success that go far beyond sailboat racing.

The America's Cup is now much more than a sailboat race. About fifteen percent of the effort goes into sailing. The rest is preparation, design, planning, fund-raising, committee work, training, building a team, logistics, and management. Winning the America's Cup involves all the elements that you need to succeed at any large, ambitious enterprise—with a fifteen percent allowance for the special skill that it takes to sail a boat around a course.

With a goal that's as big and multifaceted as winning the
America's Cup, we just can't talk about sailing as the only skill
you need. The methods I used to bring the America's Cup back
to America are the same that go into winning any other event,
prize, game, or competition. This isn't sailing. It's life.

The Art of Winning is about whatever it takes to make you
successful at whatever you do.

As I look around me and see the people who *are* successful at
this game called life, I learn more and more about the traits they
have in common. What *are* those traits? Why do some people
succeed in reaching their goals while others only half-succeed or
turn back before they really get started? What makes some people
winners?

Here are some things I've noticed:

• There *is* such a thing as a winning attitude. Maybe only a
psychologist could tell you where it comes from or why it's there,
but I do know some people have it.

• Some people regard their mistakes and defeats as indications
that they're no good or that they can't succeed, while others
stubbornly climb back up on the same bucking bronco that threw
them and hang on for dear life.

• Certain people have a mind-set that enables them to break
records, achieve the impossible, beat the odds, and dream about
things that others dare not dream.

• There is a special force—a combination of motivation, commitment, inspiration, and leadership—that gets people working
together as a team. Once that force is in action, the team is
virtually unbeatable.

• Not every winner is especially gifted. However, every winner
has the ability to optimize the talents that he or she has.

Do You Have the Desire to Win?

The desire to win is an admirable trait in human nature as long
as you have a healthy respect for the demands and temptations
that go along with that desire.

As I see it, here are some of the critical elements that comprise the *desire to win:*

- You want to see your accomplishments realized.
- You want to be rewarded for what you do well.
- You want all your hard work to pay off.
- You want the sweet thrill that comes from finishing first.
- You want to demonstrate the power of will and courage over reluctance and laziness.
- You want to prove that your imagination is stronger than all your human limitations.
- You want to show that dreams can overcome discouragement.

Winning is setting out to accomplish something even though you don't know for sure how much that effort is going to cost you in the long run. It means admitting to the world that you *want* to win, and then it's working so hard to meet your goal that you give yourself no excuse to lose. Winning is both thrilling and dangerous, because the better you become, the more you have to lose.

Winning is not a risk-free deal! Wanting to win means *being willing to risk losing.* There's no halfway. You can't take the total risk required to win big unless you can run the equal and opposite risk of *losing* big. But for anyone willing to risk both, the rewards of winning are strong and compelling.

Choose Your *Way of Winning*

The one thing I will not be able to do in this book is the one thing you must do for yourself—convince yourself that *you can be a winner.* If winning doesn't seem important to you—if the idea of giving so much and working so hard is alien to your way of doing things—perhaps you should pause for a moment to consider what winning *could* mean to you. Not everyone will win the Star Boat Worlds or be in the World Series. Not everyone can be elected to the Senate or be awarded the Nobel Prize. *But there are many other kinds of winning.* Here are some examples:

· The manager who feels as if he or she is in a rut but makes the commitment to finding a way out. He or she wants to go for an important promotion, or build a corporate team that's more effective, or look for education and training that will lead to the right spot in the corporate structure. Maybe it's time to look for another job—or rewards *outside* the job. I'll show how you can score a big win by getting *to do what you love, or to love what you do.*

· The CEO who wants to meet a five-year profit plan and succeed in delivering a promised bonus to every employee in the company. From this book he or she can learn the kind of *methodical planning* that has helped me manage complex sailing programs, small companies, and high-powered teams.

· The person who is involved in public service work, volunteer work, or a political cause that he or she believes in is critically important to the betterment of our world. Yes, you may encounter many frustrations and discouragements, but I salute your efforts, and I know what you face when you deal with committees, constituencies, and groups of people you want to influence. You have to pay tireless attention to numerous details. I'll explain *how to manage the little things that add up to a big win.*

· The amateur athlete who sets a goal of being the best in his or her league—and wins the trophy! How do you *learn to think like a winner and visualize success?* The *Stars & Stripes* team found out.

· An entrepreneur who gives up the security of a regular paycheck and steady advancement to start an enterprise with his or her name on the door. I learned to run a small business at the same time that I first learned to race sailboats, and the skills I acquired in the sport proved to be valuable in the business. And when I started my '87 Cup campaign, it was with a shoebox full of bills in the back of my interiors and drapery company. I know how frustrating it can be at the beginning, how much you have

to *believe,* and I'll tell you *how you can make your dream grow.*
· A fund-raiser who rallies people to support an important
cause. I'd like to think that motivating people to follow my lead
is one of the things I do best. *You can learn how to lead that kind
of great campaign.*

The Elements of Winning

In this book I will be introducing the five elements that I have
found essential to winning. Those elements are Attitude, Performance, Teamwork, Competition, and Goals. All the elements
are interrelated. You need a good attitude to produce a great
performance, but you also need competitive drive and teamwork.
And the only way to bring it all together is by setting goals that
you can realistically achieve.

Since these five elements are all interrelated, working on one
element may improve another element of your game. For instance, if you see yourself falling short of reaching your *goals,*
maybe the real clue to improvement is in *teamwork*—getting
together the right people who can help you reach those goals. Or,
it could be an *attitude* problem—have you really made the commitment that's necessary to be successful? Similarly, what if
you're having trouble with the *competition*—could it be your
performance that needs work?

When you're winning, *all* the elements of winning come into
play—but you're still doing it your own way. So you have to find
out what's important to you. Figure out what works for you.
Experiment until you get *all* these elements clicking together to
produce a win for yourself.

Step by Step

For me, each winning experience has been a step-by-step process
that begins with commitment and keeps building until I reach a
point where I have no excuse to lose. Here's how that process
works:

First, *I make the commitment.* It might take weeks or months to get to this first step because usually I want to consider all the reasons why I should or should not get involved. (This goes for business ventures as well as competitive sailing.) Do I have a winning *attitude* about this commitment? Can I produce the kind of *performance* that will result in a win? Can I get the people I need to create *teamwork?* Have I considered the *competition?* Are my *goals* clear to me from the very beginning?

These are questions that I try to answer honestly before I make the commitment, because I know that once I do go ahead, I won't let up. I won't turn back. I'll be *committed to the commitment.*

I go to work. I work hard and I like it. Because I've made the commitment, I don't have to look back and say, "I wonder if I *should* be working this hard . . . spending this much time . . . making these sacrifices." The hour for those kinds of doubts is past. Now it's just pure work, concentrating on all five elements of winning. I let everyone around me know what my *goals* are. I continually try to improve my *performance* so I can compete against the best. And, perhaps most important of all, I think about *teamwork*—choosing the right people, getting *them* to make the commitment, helping them reach their goals and achieve a fine competitive performance.

With great attitude and hard work, my teammates and I steadily improve. Everyone's *self-image* begins to change. We see that we're getting better prepared every day. We see our performance-level notching upward. We begin to attain goals that previously seemed unreachable, and then we surpass them. The impossible becomes possible.

Finally, *there's no excuse to lose.* At the high end of this improvement scale, my teammates and I reach a level of peak performance. Whenever we think of something that *might* go wrong, someone jumps in to fix it before it happens. If we see anything that *could* be done better, we strive to *do* it better. When a team is working at its best, every problem and every obstacle is seen as a new opportunity to come up with new solutions and better ways of doing things. No one is trying to cover up anything. No one is going to be making excuses afterward.

Run Your Own Race

I can't tell you how to run your race—whether it's in business, a profession, the arts, or athletics. But what I can do is make it easier for you to find your own way. I can show you tactics that others have used and then, as in any race, you can figure out the most advantageous tactics for *you.*

Part of the good fortune that comes to anyone who wins is the privilege of associating with winners. From my earliest days of sailing, it seems, I've had the privilege of meeting people who are winning in many different pursuits, not just sailing and sports but also business, politics, arts, entertainment, and the media. Fortunately, many of these people have been willing to make contributions to this book—articulating many things that I could not find words for myself, and showing how they've mastered the art of winning in fields outside the ones I know best.

One lesson I hope you'll learn from our combined experiences is that there is no perfect formula. Life's greatest challenges involve unforeseen wind shifts, tactical changes—accidents! *Attitude* can change the outcome in an instant. If that weren't so, I doubt that we would go out there and seek success again and again, testing ourselves, withstanding the elements, hoping for luck, and seeking out the competition both to improve and to find out who's best.

PART 1

Attitude

1

Make the Commitment

In 1983 after we lost the America's Cup to *Australia II,* not many supporters were rushing forward to support Dennis Conner's next America's Cup effort. Fritz Jewett was an exception. He and his wife Lucy had supported me in the *Freedom* campaign of 1980, and again in 1983.

Fritz is a Dartmouth and Harvard Business School graduate who served in the Navy and then went to work for Weyerhaeuser. In 1954 he moved into corporate administration at Potlatch Corp., where he became vice chairman of the board in 1977. He's a trustee of numerous foundations, including the Asia Foundation and the Pacific Presbyterian Medical Foundation. And he has supported every America's Cup campaign since 1974.

During Christmas of '83, I visited Fritz and Lucy at their home in Hawaii. Fritz told me how disappointed he'd been by the way the New York Yacht Club had treated me during the *Liberty* campaign. He said he would give me financial backing if I wanted to go out on my own and put together a syndicate that would challenge the New York Yacht Club and bring the Cup back home.

Looking back on it now, some people might say that Fritz

Jewett made a smart move supporting me when he did. But at the time it was definitely a courageous act. I had no other backers at that point. I'd never put a syndicate together before. And I was challenging the most powerful and well-financed yacht club in the United States. The New York Yacht Club had held the America's Cup for 132 years. But when it came to bringing the Cup back home, Fritz Jewett was backing Dennis Conner ahead of all the other guys.

I later found out that Fritz considered very carefully before he made that decision. He checked with people to find out whether they thought I could do the job. But once he had confidence in my reputation as a leader and an organizer of the crew, he threw his support totally behind me.

Fritz is a great manager, and it shows up in the way he conducts business. He is able to recruit top people because they know that when Fritz Jewett stands behind you he'll never let you down.

You can go ahead and do what you have to do, knowing that the man behind you is not going to waffle. He won't get cold feet. He's not going to change his mind because of back-room politics. He's *made the commitment.*

Can You Make the Commitment?

Is there a goal, a cause, or a person worthy of a commitment from you? Only you can decide. But believe me, everything becomes clearer when you do.

It takes commitment to win. If you're not committed, you won't be able to put up with the aggravation. You'll get to the point where it's just too much hassle and frustration, and you'd rather be doing something else.

Nothing you care about is going to be easy all the time. There will be dark hours when you look around and speculate about where it's all going to end. You'll wonder how you got into it in the first place. You'll think maybe you've made the biggest mistake of your life.

But if you care about the commitment, you'll come back; *if you*

don't stay committed and see it through, nothing else will make sense.
Commitment puts order in your life.
It establishes values.
It sets your priorities.
It tests all the skills you've got.
Commitment makes everything you're doing worthwhile.

Are You Ready?

How do you know when you're ready to make that commitment? Although making a commitment can be a thoughtful and well-studied process—as it was for Fritz Jewett—at a certain point you begin to see that *now is the time* to make a commitment. You can see a goal very clearly. You want to focus everything you've got on reaching that goal.

Here are what some people had to say about some major commitments they made in their lives:

A SUCCESSFUL ENTREPRENEUR: "I knew there was going to be a lot less security—and there was no guarantee of success. But I was sure I had the right idea at the right time. The market was ready for my product. All I had to do was put in that extra effort to make it happen. And I knew if I didn't take the risk then, I probably never would. It was now or never! So I decided I had to go for it."

AN AMATEUR SPORTS CHAMPION: "I was doing better and better in my class [of competition], but I was always taking time away from my family—and I wasn't putting in as many hours at my job, either. Finally, I had to bite the bullet and decide. Was I really going to go for the nationals, or was I going to hang back and never know whether I had a shot at the trophy? Once I put it that way to myself, the decision was clear. I had to make the commitment."

A BEST-SELLING NOVELIST: "I thought I had a novel in me somewhere—but writing was always a private passion. I never had time to work on it. Then I got an idea for a plot. I started to work on it. I put the book aside, worked on it some more, then put it aside again. Finally I caught a break. I was going through a job change and I had the option of taking a couple months off before my next job. I had some savings, not a lot, but enough to get by. I said to myself, 'This is your chance.' I wrote like mad for the next two months—and produced the first draft of my novel."

A LEADING CIVIC WORKER: "I get paid very little for what I do. There are more headaches than anyone can imagine. But I keep coming back, year after year. I've had the opportunity to quit, but I never do. I don't want to let people down. They're counting on me. I have two or three projects that I've started, and I'm committed to seeing them through until they run on their own or someone else can take over for me."

Yes, there is a decisive moment—a "point of no return," if you will—when you decide whether you're going to make the commitment or not. That decision may be *very* hard to make. I'm sure Fritz Jewett did some hard thinking before he decided to back Dennis Conner and take on three years of a renewed effort for the America's Cup. I'm sure that everyone who decides to go into business for himself has some sleepless nights before he decides to take the plunge into entrepreneurship. The same goes for the amateur sportsperson who has to make up his mind whether to go to for the big national trophy; the writer who risks his savings to take "time out" to finish a novel; the civic worker who continues to be dedicated to his project. *Everyone* who makes that kind of commitment does some soul-searching before they reach a decision.

But *once that commitment is made, the other decisions become easier.*

For the entrepreneurial person, it's tougher to be trapped and frustrated in a job that drains energy and provides few rewards than to take the risk and work hard to succeed. The amateur athlete who *wants* to compete gets a great rush when he starts putting in the hours of practice that he should. The novelist who wants to get published is never happier than when he finally makes the time to write. The civic-minded person who *wants* to have an impact on the community is actually relieved to make the commitment to something that really matters to him or her.

The Consequences

The fact is: *once you make the commitment, a lot of other things begin to make sense.*

Here are some things that grow out of that:

• You become focused on one act. There is a new Main Event in center ring and all the other "acts" in your life have to take place somewhere else.

• Your time becomes more purposeful. People who are committed to specific goals resist aimless activity. You become less tolerant of distractions that keep you from your purpose; you want to start seeing results.

• You rally people to your cause. Your energy and drive become more and more visible. Making a commitment is like putting headlines in the paper:

ANDREA STARTS HER OWN BUSINESS

LARRY GOES FOR NATIONAL TROPHY

JIM WRITES BIG NOVEL

JANET ORGANIZES COMMUNITY PROJECT

You draw people to your cause—people who can contribute, give advice, find resources. Your secret isn't a secret anymore. It's up there in lights. Your commitment can attract the attention of people who can really help you.

• You get surprise payoffs. You can't anticipate all the benefits that will come from making that all-important commitment. Both pleasant and unpleasant surprises may be in store—but if you've made a commitment to something that you really love to do, and you've set achievable goals, you always gain more than you lose. Yes, there are entrepreneurs who fail in business—but along the way they learn to manage people, or discover how to handle inventory, to sell themselves and their product, or to market an item. Or perhaps learn that they prefer to work in an organization. Yes, there are thousands of amateur athletes who *don't* win gold in the Olympics, but because they make the commitment they learn skills and tactics in their sport that they never would have learned otherwise. There are novelists who don't make the best-seller list and civic workers whose best efforts fail; but the writer learns something about writing a novel, nonetheless; and the civic worker may get a whole education in city planning or community organizing. The payoff in education, experience, and organization has tremendous value.

Accept That It's Impossible—and Do It Anyway

Willie Brown, the current Speaker of the Assembly of the state of California, attended an all-black, segregated school in the poverty-stricken community of Mineola, Texas. "I had a grandmother who kept telling me *there was nothing I could not do,*" the Speaker told me. "She said if I worked hard enough, I would find out what I *could* do, and I would be certain to succeed. She made me believe it!"

Willie Brown is someone who made the commitment.

"I do believe anything is possible. If you have a block, get over it simply by doing it. *Accept that it's impossible in your own mind if you wish, but go ahead and do it anyway.*"

After graduating from Mineola High School, Brown headed for San Francisco, where he worked as a janitor, shoe salesman, and playground director to put himself through San Francisco State College and Hastings College of the Law. He was admitted to the state bar in 1959 and elected to the California Assembly in 1964. In 1980, with bipartisan support, he became the first black elected as Speaker.

A highly motivated, outspoken leader in California politics, what Willie Brown has accomplished during his lifetime and his years in the State Assembly are in the category of the nearly impossible: It was nearly impossible for a black kid from a small town in Texas to get a law degree, become a state legislator, and win the Speaker's chair with bipartisan support. It's nearly impossible to pass as many bills as Willie Brown has; to speak to as many groups; to chair as many committees; and to lead as many causes. But having admitted these things are all impossible, Willie Brown *went ahead and did them anyway.*

There is only one way Willie Brown *could* make these things possible. There was only one way he would be able to put in the hard work, endure the sacrifice, and live through the disappointments these tasks entail. Willie Brown had to *care about the commitment.*

What prevents people from caring about the commitment? Many things.

For example, just when you think you're committed to some goal, people may tell you there's a faster, easier, or painless way to achieve it. Advice is cheap. If you stay tuned to every shred of free advice, you'll be likely to stray from your course many times.

But once you're committed, your internal gyroscope is set to keep you on course. You might have to work as a janitor or sell shoes to earn your law degree. You might have to ditch some aspects of your social life and put in the hours on Saturday and Sunday to get what you want. You might have to train every day for twelve years to win the race. But if you care about the commitment, nothing that you *have* to do seems like a sacrifice. In fact, following through on your commitment seems so *right* that you'll wonder how you ever operated any other way.

2

See Yourself Winning

How do you see yourself? What are you capable of doing? Can you stand in the winner's circle, accept the trophy, award or diploma, and say, "Thank you. I deserve this. I worked hard for it. I did my best and I'm glad I won"?

A lot of people have the misconception that a winner is only a winner when he gets the prize. They figure, "Why shouldn't he have a great self-image—he's won all those awards!" But the award doesn't *create* your self-image. True, the award may give you a boost. It will probably make you feel good. You'll be glad your efforts have been recognized and your hard work has paid off. You'll be glad you beat the competition. But that's not the moment when your self-image changes. Your self-image has to be strong, positive, confident, optimistic *before* you get to the top. Somewhere along the way, you have to start thinking of yourself as more than just another competitor. You have to see yourself as a winner.

Imagine Finishing First!

In 1957, two years after he and his family emigrated from Italy to the United States, Mario Andretti saw his first Indianapolis 500. As he watched the race, he began to imagine himself out on the track, taking the turns, and pulling ahead. Though he was only seventeen and had not yet raced in his first event, Andretti started to dream about winning the greatest Formula racing event in the world.

After the race was over, Mario walked out onto the track. As he looked around the empty speedway, he made a vow to himself. *Someday,* he thought, *I'm going to come here and win this race.*

A year later, in 1958, Mario Andretti won the first race he entered—a stock car race in Nazareth, Pennsylvania—in a 1948 Hudson Hornet Sportsman. In the next three years, Mario was to win twenty events in the modified stock class.

He drove his first Indy car event in 1964, starting sixteenth and finishing eleventh in a one-hundred-mile race in Trenton, New Jersey. In 1965, when he was twenty-five years old, he won his first Indy car race (the Hoosier Grand Prix), finished third in the Indianapolis 500, and won Rookie of the Year honors. In that year, he also won his first Indy Car Championship.

And in 1969—exactly twelve years after Mario Andretti had stood by himself on an empty speedway and vowed that he would win the event—he captured his first Indianapolis 500 victory.

The question is, what was Mario Andretti's self-image during those long years when he was competing in stock car and midget features? To anyone else he might have looked like just another stock car racer doing the circuit. But in his own mind, ever since a day in 1957 when he stood on the Indy race track and said to himself, "I'm going to win this event," Mario Andretti had the image of himself as *the winner of the Indy 500.*

"I didn't say it out loud," Mario told me. "If I had, people would have said, 'Here's another kid who's just dreaming. Fine and dandy.' It would have been taken lightly. I just made a vow to myself. I believed I was going to succeed.

"To be able to follow through and endure, that's what you have to do. You must have that belief in yourself. That's the *only* chance you have."

Make Mental Affirmations

Don Coryell coached San Diego State University teams to 104 wins, 19 losses, and 2 ties—a record in that school's football history. Then, in his first full season with the San Diego Chargers, the team scored more points, ran more plays, and produced more yards, first downs, and yards per play than any other team in the NFL.

I believe what sets Coryell apart is his ability to inspire a team to *make mental affirmations.*

Here's what he says about winners and losers:

"Some men consistently win, and other men with equal or more ability are chronic losers. A winner doesn't believe in losing—therefore he seldom loses. Winning is a habit that is attained by persistent mental and physical effort.

"People act like whomever they think they are. The man who thinks he will fail will ordinarily fail. A man who thinks of himself as a winner will usually succeed. . . . Your body is controlled by your mind. To a large extent, *you are what you believe you are,* and you can do what you believe you can do. . . . *Realize that the desire to be a winner must come from within.*"

If you had interviewed any crew member of *Stars & Stripes* during the months of practice in '85 and '86, any one of them would have told you that he was on a winning team. How could he believe otherwise? You don't get up at five in the morning, work out in the exercise room, and then put in fourteen-hour days of training, practice, and boat maintenance just so you can *lose!*

In his performance, in his commitment, in his mental attitude, every one on the team of *Stars & Stripes* was making mental affirmations. Every time we did well in practice, it gave us the endurance, stamina, and drive to *do better.*

Certainly we reached plateaus. And there were times when

screw-ups in the boat, the crew, or the weather dealt us setbacks. But the *affirmation* was always there, among all those guys. Every one of us wanted to do a better job the next day.

Your Self-*Image* Shows to Others

When you have a good self-image, other people can see it as well as you can. When you make those mental affirmations, your behavior actually changes. You look and act in ways that are consistent with the positive image that you have of yourself.

Consider how you appear and what you say during a job interview. Everything adds up to a self-portrait:

• *How do you come across?* How do you dress? What does your résumé look like? Have you prepared for the interview by finding out everything you can about the company? Do you know the name of the person you'll be talking to?

When you show up for a job interview you're projecting an image of who you are and who you want to be. Get that image clear in your own mind, and it will *show* in the way you dress, the way you prepare, and the way you speak during the interview. If you want to be president of the company some day, you want the people who interview you to be thinking, from the very beginning, "This is someone who's going to go a long way."

• *How do you answer questions about your expectations?* If someone asks you during the job interview, "What kind of salary are you looking for?" you should have an answer. After all, a complete self-portrait includes a salary figure, and you should have thought that through before you went for the interview. To be the person you want to be at this stage of your career, you should know what you want to be earning.

Similarly, if someone asks you what responsibilities you would like to have, or where you would like to be in two or three years, you should be able to answer quickly and easily. Those aren't difficult questions *if you have done your image-building before the interview.*

If you can say, "I want to handle new products, increase your profitability, manage a department of six to ten people, and work on new media tie-ins," your prospective employer knows he's got someone with a great self-portrait. You've spent some time thinking, *"This* is who I am and what I'm worth, *that's* where I want to be in a few years, and *here's* what I can do for this company."

· *What kinds of questions do you ask during the interview?* If you have a good self-portrait, you're going to ask your prospective employer direct, straightforward, information-gathering questions, such as:

"Where do you expect this company to be in two years?"
"Whom do you consider your biggest competitors?"
"What's been your most successful line of products?"

On the other hand, some questions indicate that *you haven't worked out your self-image yet.* For instance, suppose you ask your prospective employer:

"What kind of qualifications are you looking for?"
"Is there room for promotion?"
"When will I have my first performance review?"

These are what I call image-*seeking* questions. It's as if you're asking your prospective employer, "Gee, am I qualified; will I be promoted; will I survive a performance review?" These are questions you should be able to answer yourself. (You *are* qualified; you *will* be promoted; and your first performance review is going to be brilliant!)

· *How do you follow up?* If you see yourself being hired for the job, showing up the first day ready to go, and hitting the decks running, that attitude will show up in the interview. You will ask your prospective employer when you can expect a decision. You will set up a time to call for a decision. Then you'll follow up— thanking the people who interviewed you, sending in more information to convince your prospective employer that you're right for the job. People with a great self-image decide whether *that's the job they want*—and they go for it immediately, doing everything they can to impress their new bosses and coworkers with how hard they're going to work.

People with well-developed self-images are standouts because they begin to *live* their portraits. They carry around a clear, fully realized, vivid image of who they are now, blended with what they want to be. That's where a winning image begins.

When you have a great self-image, everything you do contributes to that image and is consistent with it. Do you see yourself as a great business leader? Then your self-image demands that you do things right. You get to the office early and work hard. You make astute management decisions. You gather exceptional people to support you and your cause, and you inspire them by example to perform at their best.

Do you want to be the greatest teacher in the world? Combine the greatest characteristics of all the great teachers you ever had. Learn your subject better than anyone else. Imagine the excitement in your classes. Create hunger for learning. Find the best students and take them farther. Find the worst students, discover what's holding them back, help them get over their obstacles, and give them something to work for.

Imagine yourself as the best, the prime example of whatever it is you want to be. Rehearse the right moves, the right thoughts, or the right words in your own mind—so when the hour comes for that action, that thought, or those words, you're prepared.

You Don't Have to Brag

If you have a good self-image, you don't have to brag about it. In fact, having that image makes it easier to remain self-confident *without* bragging, because you always know whether what you are doing is consistent with your plans.

When he was seventeen years old, Andretti saw himself winning the Indy 500. But that doesn't mean he went around bragging to every stock-car racer that he was going to be an Indy 500 winner. He just kept that image in the back of his mind, and it helped guide him when he had decisions to make.

People who have great self-images don't need to announce it to the world. In fact, the image may become more powerful because you *don't* talk about it. You can't go around every day telling your coworkers that you're going to be president of the company—*even if that's the way you see yourself.* (At best, they'd laugh at you; at worst, start avoiding you.)

Furthermore, why *should* you brag? When you start out, what do you have to brag about? You're just standing on an empty track, with thousands of miles to race before your dream is realized.

But that image directs your steps. It pulls you up again when you get knocked down. It keeps you going when you're worn out. And it helps you make choices.

In 1973, Ted Turner asked me to work in the cockpit of the new 12-meter he was preparing for the '74 America's Cup defense. I had a choice to make. Was this an opportunity I wanted? Would crewing for Ted Turner help me get where I wanted to go?

Long before I first took the helm of a 12-meter, I knew I wanted to win the America's Cup some day. To me the Cup competition was the pinnacle of international yacht racing. I saw myself, some day, crossing the finish line ahead of my challenger—and holding that silver trophy in my hands! That was my secret self-image.

So when Ted Turner asked me to come aboard, I had to ask: how does this fit into my secret plan? To answer that, I had to know what my position would be on the boat. Would that position help me toward the goal that I had in mind of winning the America's Cup? Would my self-image be intact?

At that time in my career, I was specifically looking for experience in the afterguard of a 12-meter—helmsman, tactician, or navigator—to enhance my portfolio of sailing skills.

Once I had Ted's assurance that I would be number-two man, tactician, I decided to go for it. It made sense to me. I could get the 12-meter experience I needed and find out how a Cup defense was organized. I knew that if someone has been a tactician and alternate helmsman on a winning boat, he stands a good chance of being invited back as skipper the next year.

And my self-image was that I was going to win the America's Cup some day.

The choice was obvious. I talked to my business associates, family, and a few friends about the decision, but in my own mind, it made sense as soon as I found out I was going to be the number-two man on the boat. I already saw myself at the helm. Accepting the spot with Ted just brought me one step closer to achieving my goal.

Set Your Priorities

Self-image also determines the way you operate on a day-to-day basis. What do you consider important? How do you spend your time? What are your *priority* items every day, and what items are lower down on your list? These can be tough decisions *unless* you have self-image to guide you. But if your self-image is strong, priorities fall into place, decisions become simpler. Anything that helps you toward your goal is top priority. Anything that keeps you standing still or distracts you is either secondary or entirely disposable.

When we started training for the '87 Cup, I told some of the crew, "After this, you won't be able to go back and sail those Sunday-afternoon races anymore. It won't be the same."

The reason? All the energy and concentration they'd put into getting better had created a new self-image that they couldn't throw away. They'd look at themselves and say, "What am I doing sailing a race in a halfhearted way? *This isn't the kind of sailor I am anymore.*"

Self-image is not a tyrant but a guide. It lets you do some things and not others. But by the time you get to the point where your standards have been raised, you're glad to see the unimportant things go. Having automatic priorities, dictated by your self-image, makes your choices a whole lot easier. Consider the ways a self-image guides you:

• *Should you speak up in meetings?* If you see yourself as a leader in your organization, you *have* to speak up when you have something to contribute. You can't help it. You feel compelled to introduce your ideas and insist that they be considered. Every meeting is an opportunity to rally support and cooperation from people in your organization.

• *Should you put in more hours?* If you see yourself as a success in your organization, you know the answer. You won't rest until your part of the organization is profitable, growing, and running well. If that means more hours of work—so be it.

• *Should you propose novel ideas or new plans?* If you see yourself as a creative person, you won't settle for hackneyed methods or conventional ways of doing things. You'll always search for new approaches, new directions, innovative designs, and you'll have to express yourself.

Where Psychology Kicks In

In world-class competition, winning often becomes a psychological matter.

Robert Hopkins, Jr., design test manager for the '87 *Stars & Stripes* campaign, was sailing coach for the 1984 U.S. Olympic sailing team, which out-performed any sailing team in Olympic history.

"For the average performer, ninety percent of achievement is the mechanical work you do, and ten percent is psychological. The equation shifts when you become an expert and compete against people operating at the same high skill level. Then, the psychological aspect can provide a significant competitive edge, overwhelming mechanics."

Hopkins's observation is born out of experience. Many's the race I've seen where a boat that was in the lead dropped back to second or third place and then stayed there. In those cases, the problem isn't technical. The skipper obviously has the necessary skills to win the race. The problem is psychological. That sailor just doesn't see himself as championship material. He hasn't created a winning image of himself. So when he's out in front he gets rattled, makes a mistake, or gets a little lazy. He lets a boat or two pass him, and then he feels more comfortable. He can hold position and finish in second or third. But he doesn't see himself as number one.

Self-image has a lot to do with breaking records as well as winning. In the early fifties, three track and field records were broken in the span of just a few years. Roger Bannister ran a sub-four-minute mile, Parry O'Brien put the shot better than sixty feet, and Charles Dumas high-jumped higher than seven feet.

Before those records were broken, they were considered unattainable. But afterward, there were numerous athletes who began to beat the *new* records set by Bannister, O'Brien, and Dumas.

Run a four-minute mile? It was impossible . . . until someone *did* it! After that, even high school kids started running four-minute miles.

Obviously a big part of this equation is psychological. If you see a goal as unreachable, that's probably where it will stay—just out of reach. But once you find out it *is* attainable, the whole equation changes.

Athletes like Bannister, O'Brien, and Dumas were trailblazers because they believed the "impossible" and the "improbable" *could be done.* Like Andretti, they stood on the track and said, "I see myself, some day, reaching the impossible goal." And then they went for it!

Necessary But Not Sufficient

Is self-image everything? Of course not—there's much more to winning than that. But it's the center of it all, a belief in yourself that's hard, unbreakable, and crystal-clear.

None of us is ever the *perfect* image of what we want to be. But image is always at the root of *imagination*—seeing what you want to be or do. If you can *see* yourself leading people, succeeding in business, or creating something that has never been done before, then you've already taken a first important step toward reaching your destination.

3

Incremental Improvement

Bruce Jenner, the decathlon winner who broke all records in the 1976 Olympics, trained for four years alongside gold, silver, and bronze medal winners who were living in San Jose. He created his own training schedule and, with the help of people he trained with, taught himself many of the decathlon skills. The regimen meant that he had to challenge himself constantly and make the *mental affirmations* that would keep him going.

"I saw myself standing at the bottom of a graph," he told me. "There was a straight line leading from where I stood to the place I wanted to get to, at the top. I knew the fastest way to get there was along that straight line.

"But of course it didn't go like that. There were lows and there were highs. When the lows came along, I realized I had to continue to work. And as long as I continued to work, there *would* be a high. *Because I knew I could reach the top.*"

You have to make that mental affirmation. Yes, you hit the low spots. Only *work* will get you past those to the highs. The *mental affirmation* keeps you working. You see yourself getting better and better. No matter how long it takes, or how much effort, you're going to follow that line to the top of the graph.

21

You have to wake up every morning believing that you're going to *make something get better that day.* Even if you have many distractions, set one goal that you will reach. Test an idea on someone. Complete a task. Carry out a drill. Modify a plan to suit new conditions. Raise money for your effort. Be sure, by the time you flop into bed at the day's end, that you have accomplished something! Get a little better today, and better yet tomorrow.

Look for Any Improvement!

Sometimes progress will come in small increments. At other times, you may be able to take a big leap forward. But be like Jenner: see yourself always reaching for the straight-line path to the top of your performance, driving on through the highs and lows.

How *can* you see those improvements? How can you see that you are getting better every day?

If you are a person who likes competition as much as I do, you are always looking for *measurable progress.* I've found that people who wish to reach vague, long-term goals sometimes spend too much time wishing and not enough time doing. If that's a problem, I have a simple recommendation:

MAKE A DOLLAR BET!

My dollar bets got to be famous on *Stars & Stripes.* To give a sampling:

"I'll bet you a dollar we can cut ten seconds off that jib change."

"I'll bet a dollar we're three lengths ahead of the other boat at the mark."

"I'll bet a dollar we get to the dock in seven minutes."

I've won a lot of dollars and I've lost a few. But of course I wasn't trying to win dollars—I was trying to get every guy on board to *measure results.*

Incremental Improvement

You have to find rewards where you can. Take heart from increments of improvement. You're probably not going to reach your
goal today or tomorrow—but if you can *see the progress* toward
that goal, you'll have *enough* reward to keep you going.

The farther away your goal is, the longer you have to strive to
achieve it. Along the way, you need to see *visible steps* toward
success. So you have to set levels of accomplishment for yourself.

Everyone runs the risk of being drowned in make-work, trivia,
organizational politics, procedural nightmares, and penny-ante
financial considerations. How do you digest all the necessary
procedurals without getting sucked in by them?

The key, as I see it, is to work toward *some improvement* every
day. On *Stars & Stripes* we were willing to put in weeks of design,
organization, and training just to see a tenth of a knot improvement in boat speed. With the 1987 team, I would spend hours
on the same tack, testing each of our dozens of sails. Myriad *small
improvements* in the boat's hull, rigging, sail plan, and crew work
were cumulatively the most important reason for our victory in
'87.

In business, the levels of accomplishment may be just as hard
to discern as a tenth-of-a-knot improvement in boat speed. But
if you're concentrating, and that improvement is *important* to
you, then you will see it. And you'll challenge yourself to reach
the *next* level of improvement:

- Can you accomplish in a half-hour meeting what used to be
  done in an hour?
- Will your next report or presentation be qualitatively *better*
  than the one you made last week?
- Can you increase your productivity by two percent over the
  last quarter?
- Can you increase your billing by one percent over last
  month?
- If you are a computer programmer . . . can you create a

personal library of chunks of code that you know you'll use in a variety of programs?

- If you're a salesperson . . . can you set new goals for improving the time it takes to close on a new account?
- If you manage an office . . . can you institute a better system for tracking the flow of paperwork?

These small improvements may not seem like much, but together they comprise a significant trend. If you can increase your productivity, efficiency, or profitability by a fraction of a percentage today or tomorrow, that increase—multiplied by dozens of weeks or hundreds of days—spells out radically improved results for you and your team.

Try It!

Try a one-dollar bet. Bet someone a dollar that you can wrap up an agreement by the end of the day. Bet a dollar you can settle an argument, design a new approach to a problem, put together a statement, get a chore out of the way, make a committee decision, get in touch with someone you need to talk to, or clear up a financial question.

Each of those dollar bets is a measurement of results. Reaching each goal is an increment of progress. Set up the competition and go for it! Can you keep moving forward? Can you finish ahead of yesterday? Can you *win?*

I'll bet a dollar you can.

A String of Bets

You can also apply this technique to your own activities. I like to set up a series of challenges for myself that add up to a productive day. I'll bet myself I can walk three miles, play a game of racquetball, and be ready to get on the phone to New York by seven o'clock. I'll bet I can wrap up an agreement that's been pending between Dennis Conner Sports and a sponsor. I'll bet I can clear up an employee problem in the drapery department, check in with John Marshall about a design question on *Stars & Stripes*, do a radio spot, get my car washed, meet with the Sail America board at the yacht club, and find out whether my daughter Julie has all the recommendations she needs for her college application.

Those dollar bets keep me going. Each one is a goal, a tiny increment. Each one is a mental affirmation, a competition with myself and everyone around me. Can we move this boat forward? Can we keep it going? Can we *win?*

I'll bet a dollar we can. And we will.

4

No Excuse to Lose

When you're in the middle of an important project, you probably hear a Nagging Voice from time to time.

It catches you in the middle of the night, just as you're about to fall asleep, and whispers, "You forgot to write that letter."

It wakes you in the morning, just after the alarm goes off, and says, "*Today* you have to make that phone call."

It sneaks up on you in the middle of a coffee break, and says, "You'd better begin that project *this afternoon*—or you're going to be in big trouble."

The busier you are, the louder the Nagging Voice gets, because there are more details in your life than you can manage. Even if you're putting together a string of small improvements, at times the details you've yet to handle seem endless.

But when you hear the voice—what do you do about it? Maybe you say . . .

"Stop bothering me!"

Even though you're hearing about some problem that needs to be handled or some important detail that you've forgotten, you try to put it out of your mind. You figure: Forget it. That's not important. Ignore the problem and it will go away.

Or you say . . .

"Try me later."

You postpone listening to whatever the voice is trying to tell you. Or you negotiate with yourself: "Okay, I'll make that call—but not until next week." Or you make a deal with yourself: "I'm not going to write that letter, but I'll remember to talk to the guy about it next time I see him." Or you promise yourself that you can do the impossible: "I'm not going to start that project this afternoon—but I'll come in tomorrow at four A.M. to start on it."
But if you want to win, when you hear the nagging voice you say:

"Thanks for telling me!"

That's right. The Nagging Voice is the better part of you. It's the friend giving you advice, warning you about potential problems, telling you what needs to be done. It may *seem* like nagging, but *if you want to win, you always want to hear more.* Because, if you listen to the Nagging Voice and eliminate everything that might keep you from winning, you'll have *no excuse to lose.*

Get Rid of Excuses

I once wrote a book called *No Excuse to Lose* that was primarily about sailing. A lot of sailors read that book and I think a few of them used it to figure out ways to beat Dennis Conner at his own game.

But *No Excuse to Lose* was about more than sailing tactics. That book was really about an approach to eliminating the causes of defeat that you can apply to anything you do. A lot has happened to me in the ten years since I wrote that book, but everything that's happened reinforces what I believed then and what I believe now: the best operating principle you can have is *no excuse to lose.*

No excuse to lose—that's the whip that drives everything else you do and forces you to optimize your performance.

I've seen many instances where an outstanding performance was marred by one or two easily correctable mistakes. Those mistakes almost seem intentional. And I think people make them because, when it comes right down to it, they *want* an excuse to lose.

Here's what happens when a salesperson leaves himself an excuse to lose:

P. K., vice president of sales for a general contractor, turns out a proposal for a potential client. He works hard, does his research, and meets his deadline. Then on the morning the proposal is supposed to be submitted, he dashes off a quick cover letter to the president of the client company. As P. K. is proofreading the cover letter, *a nagging voice tells him that the president's name might not be spelled correctly.* But he ignores the voice. The name looks right, so P. K. doesn't bother checking it. Instead, he encloses the letter as is and sends out the proposal.

One week later, P. K.'s proposal is turned down. Meanwhile, he's found out that he misspelled the president's name. Too late now. But whenever he wonders why the proposal was rejected, he blames it on the fact that he misspelled the president's name.

You'll Never Know . . .

What's going on here? Why didn't this guy take the extra couple minutes to check out the spelling of a name when he'd already spent weeks getting the proposal in shape? He's kicking himself for that. But *should* he be? Would someone reject a carefully prepared proposal just because his name was misspelled on the cover letter?

P. K. will never know.

But he'll always have that explanation as an excuse.

By omitting one detail, P. K. left himself open to a lot of doubt, a lot of remorse, a lot of Monday-morning quarterbacking. Now he'll always have that nagging self-doubt, knowing that with a little more care, a little more effort, he might have come out a big winner. On the other hand, maybe he didn't really want to win. Maybe he needed that open hatchway so he could always blame the loss of the sale on something else.

Why Have Excuses?

Leaving yourself an excuse is a protective mechanism we all have, to a greater or lesser degree. It's a way to lower the risk and protect your self-image. When you have an *excuse* to lose, you can always blame losing on something external to yourself. But when you have *no excuse to lose*, that means you did the best you could. Everything was perfect, but you lost anyway.

For some people, that's too much to accept. It's a blow to their self-esteem. Far better to have something, or someone, to blame, rather than pin it on themselves.

This kind of attitude can run rampant. So you have . . .

- The manager who blames his associates for failure to back him up.
- The athlete who blames his coach or his training schedule for poor performance.
- The student who says he would have done better if he'd had more time to prepare for a test.
- The creative producer who says he would be more successful if he weren't frustrated by the bean-counters.
- The entrepreneur who says his business would take off if he could afford more advertising.
- The parent who blames the school system for all the troubles a child is having.

When you hear blaming, recrimination, complaints, backbiting, or regrets, you're hearing excuses to lose. Someone's saying, "It's not my fault. I *would* have succeeded, if—"

Listen carefully to everything that comes after the "if." Nine times out of ten, you'll hear something that was preventable or correctable. A manager might blame the failure of a whole program on a minor personnel problem that could have been resolved before the program began. The athlete who says he didn't have enough time to train or didn't have the proper coaching could have prolonged his training schedule by starting earlier—or he could have found the coach who was right for him. The creative type who wants to be more successful might have to sell his ideas to the bean-counters in order to win their support.

I'm not saying you can control everything. You can't. And I'm not saying that you can win every time, because that's impossible.

But on the other hand, if there's some detail or problem that you *know about* and you can *do something about,* why not chase it down and fix it? Why should *that* become your excuse to lose?

Look for Details

Anyone who has crewed for me knows that I am a stickler for details. If I see a bolt on the mast that sticks out too far, I'll ask, "Can we cut that off?" If I find out that we might be able to use a piece of hardware that's two ounces lighter, I'll ask, "Why don't we try it out and see how it works." Then we'll test it until we know.

An extra half-inch of bolt on the masthead probably doesn't affect wind resistance in any measurable way. A winch handle that's two ounces lighter probably won't spell the difference between winning and losing. But if I knew about these things and didn't fix them, I'd have a few little excuses—and when you add up all the little excuses, you have one big excuse to lose. And I don't want *any* excuse to lose.

What Happens?

Compare the "I have an excuse" attitude to "I have no excuses." It goes like this:

I have an excuse . . .	*I have no excuse . . .*
The computer broke down just as I was finishing up.	I arranged for a backup just in case something like this happened.
The budget wouldn't allow me to produce something of really good quality.	Even though I had to go back for more money, I didn't compromise on quality.
It was a minor mistake; I thought no one would notice.	Even though it was a little mistake, it wouldn't leave me alone until I fixed it.
I couldn't convince the committee because I'm no good at speaking in front of groups.	I knew I'd have to convince the committee, so I rehearsed a lot.
My idea would have been the best, but I met a lot of resistance.	I anticipated some resistance, so I sold people on my idea before the meeting.

When things go wrong, when ideas aren't accepted, when a proposal bombs, there are *always* excuses. Plenty of them.

The odd thing is: *Most people know the excuses even before they know the outcomes.*

We tend to load up on excuses, thinking to ourselves, "Well, if I'm blamed for *this,* I'll have *that* excuse." It gives us comfort and safety.

What happens when you *eliminate* excuses? What if you try to anticipate everything that can possibly go wrong, and instead of leaving yourself open for trouble, you try to meet problems head-on before they happen?

If you do that, you don't have any excuses *left.* You're just out there performing for everyone to see, and if something goes wrong, you don't have any*one* or any*thing* to blame.

If you adopt this policy, you'll find there's a certain amount of danger in this approach, but also a lot of reassurance. You can't *blame* anyone, but on the other hand, you're doing everything you can to make things run so smoothly that you don't *have* to blame anyone.

Take your *best* excuse for losing. It could be a performance problem. It could be a personnel problem. It could be a money problem. Whatever it is, throw that excuse away. Fix it. Get it right. Don't give yourself an out. Then eliminate the next most important excuse, and the next.

Knowing you've given yourself the very best chance of winning is a great feeling. When you get to the starting line of the race, you can say, "I'm ready. I've done everything I can do up to this moment. Now I can concentrate on performing to the best of my ability."

And with the *no excuse to lose* attitude, even if you *don't* win, you still come out ahead. Because you don't have regrets. You don't need to weigh yourself down with blame, thinking "If only. . . ." No Monday-morning quarterbacking. You optimized your performance to the best of your physical and mental abilities. Your attitude was good, you worked hard, and win or lose, your proud self-image should be intact. You're ready for the next race.

That's why, if you go into one race with *no excuse to lose,* you can *always come back* for another.

5

Always Come Back

When I left Newport in the summer of 1983, I had just lost a silver cup that had been in the hands of Americans for 132 years. In the seventh and final race at Newport, *Liberty* finished forty-one seconds behind *Australia II*.

The Cup was a highly visible event. With the Americans defeating every challenge for more than a century, I think a lot of people took it for granted that the silver chalice would stay in American hands. Losing it once in 132 years isn't a bad overall record. But because everyone took it for granted that we were going to win, a lot of blame went around when we lost.

I learned a lot from that Cup, and I used those lessons to our advantage when we came back and won the Cup from the Australians in 1987. We were prepared on all fronts. Our design team was made up of the best aerospace and boat designers in the country. Our legal team was prepared to challenge designs that violated the rulebook.

Turn Lows into Highs

When Bruce Jenner was describing the lows and highs he encountered when climbing to the top, he observed:

"You never know when a low may turn out to be a high."

Every excellent performer I've ever met has had lows in his career. When it happens to you, you think it's the worst thing in your life. But when you look back, it looks more like a new beginning rather than an end.

Congressman Jack Kemp, who served in the U.S. Congress for eighteen years and never lost a congressional race, lost in his 1988 bid for the Republican presidential nomination. Just a couple of weeks after he stepped down from the primary race, he already had a new perspective on the situation:

"Sometimes losing can be the key to unlocking future victories," he observed. "In fact, losing oftentimes can be more constructive than winning because it forces us to grow and strengthen our resolve to triumph over adversity."

I agree. Yes, it's fine to win because you have a winning attitude and a fine competitive performance. But what if I had won the '83 Cup in *Liberty*, the boat we were sailing at that time? The win would have masked a very serious problem, which was that the Australians had a superior design and a faster boat. Winning that Cup would only have postponed the day of reckoning. The fact was, the United States had to narrow the design gap if we wanted to remain in the race as serious competitors.

Losing the '83 Cup taught me some of the greatest lessons I've learned—how to put together a design team, raise money, manage people more effectively, keep closer watch over the competition, and motivate people to participate in a great campaign.

When you put a loss into perspective, you begin to appreciate what it can teach you. *Instead of masking problems, it reveals them.*

Also, you never know how things can turn out if you have a

positive attitude. In this case, losing the Cup was the best thing that ever happened for both the Cup and Dennis Conner.

Stages of the Comeback

Defeat tastes awful. It always does.

But defeat is the test that every winner must face, *because no one wins all the time.*

The best way to get the bad taste out of your mouth is to begin preparing your comeback at once. Here are the critical stages in the rebuilding process:

1. Find the up-side.
2. Consider a change of tactics.
3. Do a reality check.
4. Plan your comeback.

1. FIND THE UP-SIDE

When you run into defeat, you're likely to have a run-and-hide reaction. Do you want to bury your head in the sand and pretend it didn't happen? That's natural. Who wants to stand up in front of all those people who *should* be applauding and popping champagne and say, "Well, everybody, we lost this round." This is where even the best competitors head for the locker room and try to hide from the TV cameras.

I've seen the run-and-hide reaction in a lot of people:

- The manager who didn't get the promotion he wanted.
- The student who didn't get into the school he'd chosen.
- A salesperson who didn't get the account he'd been pursuing.
- The employee who didn't get the end-of-the-year bonus he'd expected.

It might take time before you're ready to face the future. But here are some ways to speed up that process!

• Look at the people who backed you up. After '83, when I started to regroup my forces for '87, I had dozens of people who had supported my business and sailing efforts through the years. So I wasn't starting from scratch—I was starting with the core of a great new team both on land and on the boat.

• Look at your experience. You've seen frontline action. If you've had a big defeat, you've already been through the worst that can happen—so you have nothing to be afraid of. That puts you way ahead of the beginners who don't know what it's like yet.

• Look at your resources. Maybe you didn't pass the test, but you learned how to study. Maybe your business failed, but you established a loyal client base or a good track record. Maybe you learned how to motivate and manage people. Or discovered how to coordinate your efforts with those of others. As a result, you now have many more resources than when you made your previous attempt.

2. CONSIDER A CHANGE OF TACTICS

Early in your preparation for a comeback, consider a different approach. When we prepared for '87, I knew our approach would have to focus on an all-out design effort and we would have to watch our competitors more closely.

There are a lot of factors to consider when you change tactics:

• If you didn't get that promotion you wanted—find out why. Do you need more seniority? More experience? More training? It may be time to talk to someone about your future with the company and set your objectives. Is it time to change jobs, change departments, or look for new opportunities?

• If a project failed—approach the problem scientifically. Ask yourself: (1) What were my objectives? (2) Why did I fail to reach those objectives? (3) What are some other possible courses of action? (4) Which *one* course of action will give me the best chance of success next time?

When you decide on the answer to question 4, regroup your forces and go to work again:

• If you are a salesperson who didn't make a sale or get an order or a new account, list (mentally or in writing) some reasons why. For instance:

1. Didn't get to the key decision makers.
2. What I was selling didn't fit their needs.
3. My price was too high.
4. I couldn't convince them of our superior value.
5. I had trouble presenting, negotiating, or closing.

Any one of these problems can be solved in the future—either with the same account (if you have an opportunity to go back) or on your next new-account sales call. But you have to be realistic about what went wrong. Talk to people and find out if they back up your observations. In fact, you should always . . .

3. DO A REALITY CHECK

Losing out in *any* kind of competition—whether it's a dollar-and-cents loss or a blow to your ego—is an emotional experience. Some people take rejection better than others, but I don't know any seriously competitive person who can shrug it off.

That emotional reaction can skew your perception of reality. You might get into a mode of blaming yourself: "It's all my fault!" Or you might go to the other extreme and blame everyone else: "That blankety-blank so-and-so, it was a perfect opportunity and he blew it for me."

Time for a *reality check.*

Talk to people about *what* happened. Find out *why.* Hold off on the blaming part—either toward yourself or toward anyone else. Just get your facts together so your next judgment is based on reality, not speculation. For instance:

• If you didn't get the job . . . REALITY CHECK: What are the prerequisites for that position? Who made the selection? On what basis was the decision made?

• If a project failed . . . REALITY CHECK: Was it a long shot from the beginning? What were the critical steps? Was it really a failure—or a just a wrong turn that ended up teaching you something you needed to know?

• If you didn't make a sale . . . REALITY CHECK: Does your prospect have a special relationship with a competitor? Did unfavorable timing put you at a disadvantage? Is your product or service appropriate to the prospective customer?

After the competition is over and the smoke clears, you have the opportunity to observe a lot more than you could *before* the fray or *during* the heat of battle. Take advantage of that after-the-competition opportunity to do your reality check as you prepare for next time. Then . . .

4. PLAN YOUR COMEBACK

Now that you've regathered your forces, altered your tactics, and done a reality check, *plan the comeback.* All the information gathering is important in helping you to set a new time limit and formulate your objectives.

Your data may show you that you're unlikely to get that promotion in the next two years. Your reality check may indicate that you don't have the resources to be successful at a specific kind of project. A review of your tactics could reveal that you're unlikely to get *any* business from the account that you once considered a good prospect.

That's why you have to *plan your comeback.* If you go for a goal that is physically or technically *impossible* to attain in the time frame, you'll just be beating your head against the wall. If your review of the whole situation tells you that you *have* to change, then you need to be flexible enough to *make* that change before you launch a new campaign.

We all wish that defeat, rejection, and hard knocks would, somehow, never come our way. But we pick up more value from those disappointments than we'll ever find in the thrill of winning. You need some winning to build your self-image, to get that real-life affirmation. But you need some losing to discover your own limitations, broaden your range of tactics, and gather more data. And the best teacher of all is the comeback road from losing to winning that shows you that *you can do it.*

Shifting Objectives

Charles Bird Vaughan, Jr., better known as CB Vaughan, is a hero in the comeback department. In 1963, at age twenty-four, he set a downhill skiing world record by speeding down a mountain in Portillo, Chile, at 106 miles per hour. But the next year, he did not even make the Olympic ski team. For the fastest downhill racer in the world, that was a major defeat.

CB planned his comeback, but it wasn't in downhill racing. Though he spent the next four years on the pro racing circuit in Europe, and worked for AMF Sports for a short time, his comeback really began when he decided to start his own skiwear company.

CB didn't know anything about apparel design. He had never cut out a pattern or sewn a seam. He had no suppliers, no designers, no marketing team, no outlets, and no expertise in the clothing industry. But CB Vaughan thought he could design a pair of warm-up pants that would be better than anything on the market.

In 1969, Vaughan read a book on pattern making, drew some ski pant designs, and approached contractors about making high-performance warm-up pants for skiers.

"They looked at me like I was really bizarre," says Vaughan.

When he couldn't work out a satisfactory contract with any of the established companies, Vaughan decided to begin manufacturing himself. He invested $5,000 in supplies, hired three part-time seamstresses in Bennington, Vermont, and began cutting and stitching. He knocked on the doors of ski shops and sports stores throughout New England and sold out of the trunk of his car. Gross sales in 1969 were $67,000. In '70, he got $50,000 from a banker and introduced three new garments—a knitted ski hat, a racing shell jacket, and a ski parka.

CB Sports was on its way.

Today, CB Sports is a $40-million sports apparel company. Headquartered on a twenty-five-acre site in Glens Falls, New York, CB Sports also has manufacturing facilities in Bennington, Vermont; North Adams, Massachusetts; and Salem, New York, employing approximately 465 people.

Over the years, CB Sports has encountered all the problems of a rapidly growing company—under-capitalization, problems of meeting demand, headaches of constantly introducing new products while keeping up inventory. But the guiding principle of CB's career has become the guiding principle of his company: *always come back.* That attitude is infectious. When you're dealing with CB Sports, every problem is solvable, every demand can be met—nothing is too difficult!

CB is constantly setting new goals and new directions for CB Sports. Combined with his always-can-do attitude, he is a great salesman who believes in the quality of his products. And because his energy is a spur that drives everyone in the company, dealing with his employees is like dealing with CB himself. As a result, even in years when skiwear sales have plummeted, CB Sports has grown.

This is CB's victory, snatched from the jaws of defeat—and from the disappointment of not making that '64 Olympic team.

"When you are successful at the majority of things you've done, you begin to take things for granted," he says. "The lesson I learned as an athlete was that the reality of defeat could become a motivating factor. By the time I was twenty-six or twenty-seven I had gone as far as I was going to go. I had to say there was something else for me besides the winner's circle—and that was the beginning of CB Sports."

When CB Vaughan made the decision to get out of professional downhill skiing and into the clothing business, he created a whole new set of objectives. His plan was ambitious. It was long-range. But the objectives he set for himself were *attainable,* as he proved.

A Kick in the Guts

It won't get any easier. It will probably get harder. That's why you have to like the challenges, the competition, the thrill of winning. And sometimes, even with all that going for you, you still get a good kick in the guts!

In his first season with the Yankees, Mickey Mantle had a horrible batting slump. He couldn't hit anything. In a double-header against Boston, Mantle struck out three times in the opener and twice more in the second game. His coach, Casey Stengel, finally pulled him from the lineup.

A few weeks later, playing in Kansas City, Mickey got a call from his father. Mantle told his father he was planning to quit pro ball.

Five hours later, after a late-night drive all the way from Spavinaw, Oklahoma, Elvin Clark Mantle stalked into his son's hotel room and gave him hell.

"So you've had your slump," Mickey's dad said. "You're not the first and you sure won't be the last. Everybody has them, even DiMaggio. Take my word. It'll come together. You'll see."

Mickey Mantle promised his dad he would give it another try.

During the next forty games, he hit eleven home runs and fifty RBIs, for a .361 average.

The Chump Factor

"In our sport, one weekend you're a champ and the next weekend you're a chump."

That's Danny Sullivan, another Indianapolis 500 winner. In 1985, while racing on the Roger Penske team, Sullivan passed Andretti inside the yellow line, lost control on the curve, did a 360-degree spin, recovered, went on to overtake Andretti twenty laps later, and won the Indy.

"In the next ten races," Sullivan recalls, "I led in every race—and I lost every race because of some problem. In those ten races, we had five things break that, in the history of Penske Racing, had never broken before. When a couple of those things happened, I was so far in the lead it was a joke."

Surviving that, Sullivan came back to train harder than ever. In his first three years on the CARG/PPG Indy car circuit, he had seven victories.

"Having won Indianapolis, the motivation was the *victory*. The smell of success was so great that I wanted it worse than ever. You realize you want it—but you don't realize how much it really means to you until you get it. And once you get it, you say, 'Oh, boy, I like this feeling of *winning*.' "

Back to Work Again

There isn't a single kind of defeat, discouragement, or disappointment that some winner has not experienced at some time. What can you do except go back to work again? Let the shock wear off. Go through the blur of disappointment. Shift your strategy—but don't abandon your goals. Though winning may seem far away at times, the experience of losing is only a setback, never the final word.

PART 2

Performance

6

Dare to Meet the Best

One of the greatest supporters of the *Stars & Stripes* effort was Mike Dingman, head of the Henley Group.

Mike started his career as a factory trainee with Pfaff & Kendall, a Newark, New Jersey, manufacturer, then went with an electronics firm in Braintree, Massachusetts. At age thirty-three he joined the Wall Street firm of Burnham & Company (now Drexel Burnham Lambert Incorporated) as an associate in corporate finance. At that point his career really powered up.

Within four years he was general partner at Burnham, and a year after that he left Burnham to organize Wheelabrator-Frye. Dingman put the company together in 1970, headed it up for the next thirteen years, and under his leadership Wheelabrator became one of the most phenomenal corporate success stories of all time. By 1983 Wheelabrator was the 209th largest corporation in the United States, with 20,000 employees and 75,000 stockholders.

Today, Mike Dingman is managing director, chairman of the board, and CEO of the Henley Group, a diversified multinational company with more than eight billion dollars in assets.

(Wheelabrator, the company he created, is just one of those assets.)

I first met Mike in 1984, when we started getting organized for the '87 effort, and he helped Sail America and the team of *Stars & Stripes* through some of our darkest hours. Mike showed tremendous courage and conviction by backing our effort at a time when we were deeply in debt, struggling to fund a new design, build a boat, and launch a campaign to bring the Cup back home to America.

I began to realize the extent of Mike's great personal power when he started calling up CEOs all across America and asking for their support in our all-out effort. These were *the best people there were,* and Mike had surrounded himself with them throughout his career. When the call went out, they responded.

Mike's secret?

"Always associate yourself with people more competent than yourself—*and go for the best!*"

Find the Top Performers

Those words are significant to anyone who wants to combine a winning *performance* with a winning *attitude.* You have to *look for the best,* then do your darnedest to associate with them. Work with them, watch them, learn from them. For a businessperson, this means finding the people who are the greatest at whatever it is they want to do—start a company, manage people, buy and sell assets, or introduce new ideas and new products to the market. You won't win by associating with people who go for the quick fix, the easy way out. Inevitably those methods backfire and if you're not lucky, you get caught in that backfire. What can you learn from second-raters and nonwinners? How to *be* second rate and how *not* to win.

When you find out who the *best* are, watch what they're doing and learn from them (their mistakes as well as their victories!). If possible associate with them. You'll find out more about winning than you ever dreamed possible.

Search Them Out—Find Out What They're Doing

When I started sailing, the *best* sailors were just names to me, but I knew I wanted to associate with them someday. I wanted to meet Paul Elvstrom, the Danish sailmaker and boatbuilder who had won four Olympic gold medals, two Star World Championships, two Soling World Championships, and a Half Ton World Championship. I dreamed of racing against great sailors like Lowell North, Ted Hood, and Buddy Melges. Later on, when Ted Turner was at the peak of his 12-meter racing career, I knew that I wanted to race with him or against him (as it turned out, I did both).

From the beginning, I couldn't hear enough about them. *Why* were they the best? *What* were they doing better than anyone else? *How* did they train and practice? What were the exceptional qualities they had that made them so special? What did they do to their boats and their sails? What were their tactics?

As soon as I heard about something they were doing that might work for me, I tried it out. I copied their methods to find out if they worked for me—then adapted those methods to my own style. I learned, I practiced. I seized every opportunity to meet them or to test my skills against theirs.

In starting my businesses, I have tried to learn from the best in business. I'll readily admit that I've tried to pick up everything I could from Mike Dingman, because I think he's the best there is at managing people and assets and running a huge company. When he says I should meet someone or talk to someone who has expertise in a particular area, I *go*, because I know I can't get better advice anywhere else.

In fact, getting ready for the 1988 America's Cup was a whole new learning process. When we made the decision to meet the '88 Kiwi Challenge in a catamaran, *I'd never raced catamarans!* So I had to learn—and I wanted to know, "Who are the best catamaran sailors in the world? Who's designing cats that are lighter and faster than anything afloat?"

I asked catamaran sailors, boatbuilders, sailmakers. I asked people I met on airplanes and people who wrote me letters offering help. When the same names started to come up, I got in touch with those people. By March of 1988 I was learning catamaran sailing from the best catamaran sailors in the world, with the best designer of the tricky solid-wing rig showing me how to handle a kind of sail I'd never used before.

Where Will You Find the Best?

If you want to win, you have to begin by asking, "Who are the best? Where are they? How can I meet them? How can I learn from them and compete against them?"

- If you fly model airplanes, wouldn't you like to compete against the best model-airplane flier in the world?
- If you decide to be a surgeon, don't you want to learn your skills from the best surgeons practicing today?
- If you're taking up guitar, don't you want to get started with the best guitar teacher you can find?
- If you're going to study astronomy, don't you want to associate with the best astronomers in the country and learn how *they* do it?

There are at least three steps to identifying the best people and benefiting from their contact, performance, advice, and knowledge:

1. Find out who they are. On my way to a speech at the Harvard Law School Forum, I spoke to a student who was considering a career in judicial law. When I asked her to name the best judges in the country, she answered immediately, naming a judge in Washington, another in Baltimore, and a third in San Francisco. She talked about the importance of some of those judges' recent decisions and described their significance in the legal community. The student said her goal was to do her clerkship with one of those three judges.

So the first step is to find out: *Who* are the exceptional people in your field? What are their backgrounds? What qualities make them exceptional? Find out everything you can about them.

Don't settle for second best! When you're at the low end of the totem pole, you might think, "I could never work for that guy—he's too high-powered," or "She's a lot more talented than I am—way out of my league."

It's always that way when you're starting out. The first time I met the championship Star boat sailors, I thought, "Those guys are incredible. They're gods." Bruce Jenner told me he felt the same way the first time he met gold medal-winning Olympic athletes. How could he ever train against those people? It was awe-inspiring just to shake their hands.

But even if they seem unreachable—too important, too talented, or too busy to pay attention to you—put them on your list! Those are the people you want to associate with. Now you have to find a way to do it.

2. Get close to the best. The law student who already knows where she's going to apply for a clerkship has the right idea. But if you're not in a career or profession where the application-and-recommendation process is straightforward, you may have to use some ingenuity. Here are some ways to go at it:

· Move near them. Bruce Jenner moved to San Jose, where a number of Olympic athletes were in training. He started training alongside them. Pretty soon, the pedestal they were on didn't seem so high anymore. He was learning from his idols—and competing against them.

· Use social contacts. If you want to meet the best people in your own organization, seize every opportunity to get to office parties or meetings where they'll be. You might have to push to get an invitation. But you're not just going to be entertained. You have a mission: you have to *meet* those people. (And don't be shy about this mission, either—ninety-five percent of the people at that party are there for precisely the same reason.)

· Make professional contacts. Find reasons to do business with the best people in your profession. If there's an organization in which they're prominent, join, seek them out, find out what you can do to help.

• Do something different from everyone else. The best way to get close to the best is to make their life easier in some way—and I don't mean just bringing them coffee. I know an accountant who always sent two copies of the same financial report to the president of his company. One copy was unmarked. The second was highlighted with his own marks, and he always attached a short, typed note with his own two-sentence (unsolicited!) opinion. The president got into the habit of turning to the marked-up report first—he could get through it faster, hit all the important points, and save himself the time and trouble of going through columns of figures to get to the key points. (Today, that accountant is chief financial officer of the company.)

• Personal contacts. Find out *who knows* the person you want to meet. Can a friend arrange a meeting for you? People who *know* important people usually like to talk about them. Find out everything you can—and see what your friend or friend of a friend can do about setting up a meeting. (Mike Dingman was a friend of a friend!) If your contacts can suggest ways to get close to the people you want to meet, by all means, *take their advice.*

3. *When you meet the best, have a hook ready.* An opportunity to meet an outstanding person is an opportunity to begin an association that could last a lifetime—*or* could be forgotten in the next ten minutes. It all depends on *whether you have a hook ready.*

If you want the attention of someone you work for, don't hesitate to ask for advice or counsel. Henry Rogers, chairman and founder of Rogers & Cowan Public Relations, observed that upper-level people have several motivations for listening to up-and-coming people in the ranks and helping them along:

• They can win points with *their* superiors for helping people along.
• They build supporters in the rank-and-file of the company.
• And they can get information about "how things are going at the bottom."

I know from my own experience that I'm willing to answer anyone's questions as long as: (1) Those questions are relevant to the business we need to get done; (2) It's clear that the person to whom I'm talking is going to *do something useful* with the information, advice, or answers I give; and (3) He's trying to get ahead and learn on his own, not just suck up to the guy in charge.

Suppose you're talking to someone who is one of the best in your own company and you know you're going to want his advice in the future. If you only have the chance to ask *one* good question, it might go like this:

"I'm considering (some new idea or project). When I get further along on this, can I ask you a few questions?"

(Why *shouldn't* he agree? It'll give him a chance to find out what you're working on and spend a few minutes with you—no strings attached.) Or:

"I have to meet with (the name of someone important) next Tuesday, and I think it's going to be a critical meeting. Could I go over the plan with you before I talk to him?"

(If the person you name is important to the success and future of the company—then of course!)

But what if you want to establish a hook with someone who isn't in your own company or business? Often I meet experts in other fields. I want their advice. In fact, it might be critical that I get in touch with them at some time. If I leave without a hook, there's a chance that I might have a difficult time finding that person when I need him. So I'm straightforward about it:

"Do you ever do consulting? I might need you. How can I get in touch?"

(At that point I want to get a card—and even better, a home telephone number.)

But what if you're meeting someone you want to work for? You're certainly not going to be hired on the spot, no matter how brilliant you look. What's your hook for meeting that person later—or working with him?

First of all, if he's really as good as you think he is, then he's *looking* for eager people with a great attitude—people like you! And if you've done your research and asked around before you met him, then you know what that person is working on. Figure out where you might fit in. What can you offer?

John Grant—better known on our team as "Rambo"—was a twenty-year Marine Corp man (he'd served in Vietnam in the infantry) when I met him over dinner back in 1983. We got into a conversation and I realized that with his military background he knew a lot more than I did about transporting large objects over long distances. It so happened, at that time, I was in the early phases of figuring out how to transport a very large object (a 12-meter sailing vessel, to be exact) over a very long distance (all the way to Australia). I plied John with so many questions about logistics that I think he realized immediately he could be useful to me and my team in the upcoming America's Cup.

After our discussion over dinner I might never have heard from him again. But about a week later, he sent along some sketches and information related to what we'd been talking about. It was all valuable stuff.

So when we needed someone to handle that side of things, John Grant was my choice.

If you have expertise in a specific area, figure out how you can help. Find out where you can make a contribution. Demonstrate your follow-through technique.

Follow Through

Do these approaches *work?*

Yes, but only if you have a real interest in what the best people are doing. You have to respect the limitations on their time. *Contact for the sake of contact* is bogus—and anyone in a high-powered venture is going to see through it. You have to really *want* to help out, to learn, to grow, to make your contribution.

If that attitude shows up in your performance—as it did with John Grant—people will appreciate the contribution that you make.

So it's more than finding a hook. You also have to follow through by *performing* your best.

7

Do Your Homework

Homework doesn't come *before* performance.

It's *part of* performance.

Performance begins when you start to prepare for action—in business, in sports, in education, or anything else you want to do well. Consider:

- Do you want a securities broker who hasn't researched the companies he wants you to invest in?
- Do you want an athlete on your team who doesn't know the rules and plays of the game?
- Do you want a surgeon who hasn't kept up with the latest techniques in surgery?
- Do you want a program designer who is using software that's five years out of date?

For anyone who wants to excel in anything, you can never do enough homework, never have enough information. You shouldn't be satisfied until you have tapped every resource that might improve performance.

Find Out What's Relevant—and Use It

Doing your homework doesn't mean you have to turn into a college professor.

Chuck Yeager was a lousy student, but a great researcher where it counted.

More than once, Yeager came close to flunking his classroom courses for being a test pilot. He hated the math and he had to be tutored through the theory. If it hadn't been for his mentor, Colonel Boyd, who intervened for him with more than one instructor, Chuck Yeager would probably be sitting in a classroom today, still trying to figure out logarithms.

But logarithms didn't affect performance. Flight manuals did. And Yeager was interested in performance. He studied the manuals until he knew them backward and forward. Somewhere in the fine print of each manual was information that might save his neck and save the aircraft. Studying those flight manuals was just as difficult as learning logarithms, but a lot more practical. He wasn't learning theory; he was learning to fly better.

Doing his research wasn't just homework—it was a matter of life and death.

Yes, research can be dull. Chuck Yeager did not necessarily enjoy reading new aircraft handbooks. But if he hadn't studied them carefully, he probably would not be alive today.

Doing your homework may not be a life-or-death issue for you. *But it is definitely a win-or-lose issue.* Because if you want to turn in a winning performance, you definitely have to do your research.

Hate Research?

I know why:

- It can reveal something you'd rather not see—some area of your own performance that needs improvement. Perhaps a weakness in your team or an unexpected strength held by your competitor.

- It may create additional costs—and you have to finance that.
- It can give you an answer you don't *like*—or tell you something that contradicts your gut response to a situation.
- What you discover can make more work for yourself—or at least it might seem that way.

But keep in mind:

- Research is preparation—and every hour you spend in preparation can save two or three hours in execution. A quick, uninformed decision early in the game can send you up the wrong branch of a decision tree. Research is no guarantee against this—but it's the best protection you have.
- It reveals your competitor's strength. If you know that before the game, you have a chance to change your tactics or compensate for weaknesses in your performance. If you don't find out what he's got until the middle of the race, it could be too late.
- It gives you bad news ahead of time. If you're planning to buy a company, wouldn't you prefer to know it's unprofitable *before* you buy it? Even if you're gambling on a long shot, don't you want to know your percentages before you put your money down?

Research isn't a luxury, it's a necessity. However, research *has to be controlled*—it should not control you. If you don't maintain control, you'll never get the work done on time.

Know the Questions

Great research is *thought* and *action*. The thought part of it is:

Figure out which questions to ask!

The *action* part is:

Find the answers!

In scientific research, many of the answers come when the researchers figure out which questions they should be asking. Piles of data are compiled—hours of research, experimentation, testing, theorizing, and evaluating—all to find out the right questions.

No matter what field you're in, you have to start by figuring out the right questions to ask. This is true whether your subject is:

- Technology
- People
- Organizations, or
- Money

For example:

IN TECHNOLOGY . . .

- What can this material (machine, device, method) *do for me?*
- Under what conditions has it been tested?
- What happens to it under maximum stress?
- Is it operator/user friendly?
- What do we have to do to maintain it?
- How do we get it fixed if it breaks down?
- What can we do with it that's never been done before (what are its capabilities)?
- How do we test it for those new capabilities?

WITH PEOPLE . . .

- What's his past experience?
- What's the toughest thing she's ever done?
- Did he get where he is by himself or did someone else pave the way for him?
- What's her attitude like?
- How does he take criticism?
- Whom did she work with in the past?
- Has he come up with any new ideas recently?
- Why did she leave the place where she was before?
- What does he want to be when he grows up?

ABOUT ORGANIZATIONS . . .

- Who really makes the decisions in that company?
- How many people must we deal with in order to get things done?
- What's the corporate culture like? (Competitive? Innovative? Cautious? Image-conscious? Bottom-line oriented? Entrepreneurial? Bureaucratic?)
- What makes people in that organization look good?
- Who (or what) are they scared of?
- Who are their heroes?

ABOUT MONEY . . .

- What are other people charging for this type of product/ service?
- What kinds of margins are they working with?
- What kinds of margins are *we* working with?
- What explains the difference (if there is one)?
- What return on investment are they/we getting?
- How long will it take us to make money if we take on this venture?
- How can we speed up the return on investment?
- What are our future options?
- Where are the hidden costs?
- What are the risks? Liabilities?
- What increased value can we give our product or service that will allow us to charge more?
- What do we want from a negotiation?

The preparations for every America's Cup involved all these areas—technology, people, organizations, money. I asked thousands of questions, and so did everyone who worked with me. We searched out people who had the knowledge in these areas (naturally we looked for *the best*), and when we found them, we went into action with all the questions we'd stored up.

Questions are the *core* of research. When you begin to ask good questions, you are starting to improve your performance. And those questions can save miles of long-distance travel in the wrong directions.

The great thing about doing your homework is that *you don't have to know everything.* All you have to do is know the right questions to ask—and then ask them!

Portrait of a Great Researcher—Part 1

John Marshall, who brilliantly coordinated our design team's efforts for the '87 Cup, was back in '88 for the defense against the New Zealand challenge. John is thorough, thoughtful, and has a highly analytical mind. A graduate of Harvard (where he majored in biochemistry, not engineering!), he is the former president of North Sails, and he has the practical advantage of extensive sailing experience, particularly in many America's Cup defenses. He was instrumental in both the *Freedom* and *Enterprise* campaigns.

In the '87 campaign, John immediately identified the limitations of tank-testing hulls, which had been our primary method of designing 12-meters up to that time. John saw that when you translate a small-scale model into a full-scale boat, there is a great deal of room for human error in setting up the mechanics. He realized that if we were to surpass the Australians in our design, we would have to use computer modeling. That would allow us to test a wide range of data before we began building any models at all—data that included meteorological conditions, information on lift and drag, the integration of hull and keel, various building materials, and other factors.

The computer allowed the design team to test many of these variables with the greatest possible efficiency. At the same time, John put together an experienced, innovative, and creative research team by combining the talents of Britton Chance, Bruce Nelson, and Dave Pedrick.

It took John Marshall and his team nearly a full year to come up with the design that proved to be the final *Stars & Stripes*. Waiting that long for a boat almost killed me. But I knew the time was well-spent. The research had to be done.

We had to develop a boat that was as good as *Australia II* and then surpass that design with another boat specifically built for conditions in Australia.

We knew we were going to have to meet a whole new set of conditions. In Newport, where we sailed in '83, winds are generally light to moderate—the equivalent of San Diego. On the west coast of Australia between Perth and Fremantle, where we would be meeting the defender, there was a strong sea breeze called the "Fremantle Doctor." We expected that the winds would be relatively mild in October and November when the round-robins began. But we expected tougher conditions in December, and by January we could expect the "Doctor" to blow from fifteen to thirty-five knots with seven- or eight-foot sharp seas coming in off the Indian Ocean.

So *Stars & Stripes* had to be built for the strong winds and high waves that we would encounter in February when we sailed the Cup. At the same time, it had to perform well enough in moderate winds to get us through the round-robins, semifinals, and finals before we actually met the defender.

In the end, we built three boats.

All of them had the wing keel that the Australians had put on *Australia II*, and from the very beginning we knew we were faster than her. The modifications that we made on *Stars & Stripes '83* and *'85* were improvements: we changed keels, moved the rig around, and changed rudders. Then we built *'86* with a double bow—a flat section under the bow, with a bump at the waterline. Finally, John Marshall combined everything we had learned about hull shape, waterline length, deck layout, and keel configuration to come up with *'87*.

All the research and planning that went into those three boats proved decisive. There were many tense moments in the early races when moderate winds favored our competitors. But when we finally faced the Australian, *Kookaburra III*, for the Cup races, there was no question who was faster. We were still vulnerable in light air, but as soon as the "Fremantle Doctor" got up to fourteen knots or so, we were fine. In all four races, we never finished less than one minute ten seconds ahead of *Kookaburra*.

Portrait of a Great Researcher—Part 2

The America's Cup '88 presented yet another set of challenges— new design problems and new research.

In July 1987, about six months after our victory in Australia, New Zealand merchant banker Michael Fay announced his challenge against the San Diego Yacht Club, holder of the America's Cup. Fay and his lawyer found a loophole in the Deed of Gift. They claimed the right to challenge in a monohull (i.e., a boat with a single hull) with a ninety-foot waterline.

The boat was larger than anything being raced in the United States—or anywhere else, for that matter. The New Zealanders knew that at the time of the challenge. In fact, their own boat was in the design stage when they announced their intention to go for the Cup.

In November 1987, the Kiwis challenged us in court, and the New York judge gave them the green light.

When the Kiwi's challenge was upheld, we had two choices— to meet them in a boat of similar design or to come up with an alternate (and, we hoped, faster) type of boat for the defense. We went for a design using two parallel hulls linked together—a catamaran—and by December 1, 1987, we had started a radically different kind of *Stars & Stripes* plan that we hoped would defeat the Kiwis off San Diego.

Faced with a totally new set of design problems, John Marshall started research with his usual energy and thoroughness. The challenge this time was to design and build a multihull boat in under five months. To accomplish this, John had to put together a team that would represent the practical, hands-on experience of catamaran designers, along with people who could computer-design the models and calculate the loads on superlight materials.

The new *Stars & Stripes* had to be larger than any multihull currently in use for shore racing. It would have to be extremely lightweight to perform well in the light to moderate winds of southern California. And its sail inventory would include a "wing design"—more like a light, rigid, vertical airplane wing than a conventional sail. The design was totally innovative; the time-crunch horrendous.

John quickly put together a new team of advisors that included a specialist who had worked with C-Class (25-foot catamarans with solid-wing rigs) and Formula 40s (40-foot catamarans with conventional sails), as well as a seagoing maxi-cat designer. Consultants recruited from around the country included an Olympic medalist in the Tornado class and a multihull ocean racer. For expertise in high-tech composite construction, John turned to Scaled Composites, Inc., headed by Bert Rutan—the same company that designed the superlight *Voyager* airplane that made the first nonstop circumnavigation of the world.

Faced with an extraordinary challenge, John Marshall's team did their research under high-pressure conditions and produced the results we wanted. The boat they created made our Cup defense possible within the given time and money constraints.

Let Research Guide You—Not Stop You

Research increases your knowledge of your own game, it helps you understand your competitors, it gives you greater flexibility. True, some people may get bogged down in the research itself. It's possible to explore too many "if . . . thens" and "what happens in case . . . ?" But if you keep the end goal fixed in your mind, research won't *stop* performance. It will *guide* performance. And when it does, you will find your performance improves radically.

8

Prepare a Strategy

All the work that goes into doing your homework also helps you *prepare a strategy*.

Senator Pete Wilson of California cut his teeth in politics working in the State Assembly of California and in the San Diego mayor's office. While he was in San Diego, Pete Wilson had a major impact on the city's progress, winning national attention with the programs he led—crime-fighting, land management, political reform, and budget management. When he became U.S. senator in 1983, he had already taken a stand regarding one of the nation's foremost issues—a balanced budget amendment to the U.S. Constitution. Recently, Senator Wilson told me how he goes about *preparing a strategy:*

"I think it is tremendously important to very carefully assess the situation and then chart your course. In any adversarial situation, you have to think ahead and be prepared to respond to your competitor's next move."

In advocating a balanced budget amendment to the Constitution, Senator Wilson had to plan two possible strategies simultaneously—one that depended on congressional support of the amendment, the other relying on state support of a constitutional convention. When the amendment proposal did not get the two-thirds majority it needed from both houses of Congress, Senator Wilson was prepared to take the measure directly to the states.

"You can't just passively set your course and then *not* react to changed circumstances," he observed. "You should have a strategy that accommodates and responds to change. You shouldn't have to react at the last minute as the result of having been surprised."

Plan Ahead—In Detail

Whether you're advocating a constitutional amendment, preparing for sports competition, planning a marketing campaign, launching a new company-wide program, or preparing for a meeting, you have to *prepare a strategy*. But that strategy should leave room for change.

Some people can prepare mentally. Others talk it out. Or chart it out. Or write it out. The secret isn't *how* you strategize. The secret is to *do* it, as thoroughly and completely as possible, trying to eliminate all surprises.

• In Pete Wilson's case, his strategy for passing a constitutional amendment is based upon Article V of the Constitution, which states that an amendment can be initiated by the Houses of Congress or by the states. From the very beginning of his campaign, Senator Wilson was prepared to use either strategy, *even though his goal remained the same*. When both Houses of Congress failed to pass the balanced budget amendment, Senator Wilson was immediately prepared to put his second plan into action.

• In the case of *Stars & Stripes '87*, I had three years to prepare the strategy for winning—and prepare it again and again and again—*before any race took place*. I tried to see the competition completely, in every detail—the tactics I would use in particular situations, the performance of the boat and crew. And before each race, we thoroughly reviewed the performance-to-date of each competitor and shifted our tactics accordingly. We didn't want any surprises.

• For *Stars & Stripes '88* we had to prepare a number of strategies simultaneously. Whenever Michael Fay tried a new legal tactic or suggested a change in the America's Cup challenge, we had to run through the whole scenario again with a new script and discuss the various contingencies and possibilities with everyone who would influence the outcome of the competition.

Mental Prep

Mental preparation for the whole sequence-to-come is an essential part of performance. Any time you reach toward a goal, you have to think through contingencies and develop a thorough strategy that embraces other plans *just in case.* The better prepared you are for contingencies, the more confidence you're likely to have in your performance. If Plan #1 doesn't work, *you're prepared* with an alternate course of action.

Consider how this kind of strategizing can affect an important presentation that you have to give before a live audience. That audience might be a group of your coworkers, a committee, a potential client, or a review board—the problems of giving an effective presentation are similar in each situation. For instance, here are some of the contingencies you might have to prepare for:

1. What if someone in the group raises an objection?
2. What if someone asks for evidence you don't have?
3. What if your audience becomes bored?
4. What if the group votes down your ideas, your proposal, or your recommendations?

All these are real possibilities, so you don't gain anything by pretending they don't exist or by hoping they won't happen. In fact, you'll be far more confident in your presentation if you *prepare for a change of course.* For instance:

1. Prepare to encounter objections. List all the objections you can think of. If you're an architect presenting a plan for a commercial building, your clients might object to cost, layout, or any number of other variables. As part of your plan-ahead strategy, you'd have to meet with people individually or with groups from each department. *Ask* what they think of the plan. *Seek out* their objections. Then *prepare* to meet those objections appropriately during the meeting.

2. *Prepare the evidence.* If you think someone in the group might ask you for facts, statistics, or information, plan your strategy accordingly. Be prepared to back up your case. If there's some fact that you don't have at your fingertips, anticipate how you will reply when someone raises that point. (An honest "I don't know"—followed by a direct explanation of why the information is unavailable to you—is undoubtedly your best reply.)

3. *Prepare to gain your audience's attention.* Whether your presentation is five minutes or five hours long, you have to plan how you will change the course of the meeting if people begin to lose interest. Just plodding ahead, in this situation, is the *worst* thing you can do. Some other possible courses of action:

- In a small group, mention someone *by name.* It's an instant way to get the attention of that person as well as everyone else in the room.
- Be prepared with examples that are relevant to everyone in the audience.
- If it's appropriate, get other people to participate in the meeting, so yours isn't the only voice they hear.
- Ask for responses from your audience and then make sure their questions are answered.
- Use presentation aids (audiovisuals, etc.) to add variety.
- Be flexible in the program, so you can call for a break, cut the meeting short, or change the agenda if you're losing your audience.

4. *Prepare for a "no" vote.* If you're presenting a proposal, it *could* be rejected. If you're trying to close a sale, you *might* get a "no" at this meeting. If you're looking for acceptance of an idea or a plan, it *could be* tabled until the next discussion. So, part of

your planning should include a strategy that you can use in case the vote goes against you. Here are some possible strategies:

- Plan to propose a "next step" that leaves communication open.
- Suggest another time when you can meet with the group to present a revised proposal.
- Get everyone to agree to *one part* of your plan with the understanding that you will further develop the other parts of the program in response to their concerns.
- Be prepared to close the presentation on a positive note, even if your plan, proposal, or idea has been rejected. No matter what the outcome, everyone in that meeting should feel good about you and what you have to offer.

The first time you run the presentation in your own head, some of the details may be fuzzy. How *will* you respond to objections? What *are* your strategies if you meet resistance or lack of interest or if you're voted down? Imagine the worst that can happen as well as the best, so you're prepared for anything.

As the date approaches when you have to turn your mental preview into a real-life performance, *you should clear up these details.* Every time you preview the presentation, it should become more and more vivid.

One by one, fill in the details. Prepare your visuals and practice using them while you rehearse your talk. Figure out responses to possible objections. Talk to people who will be there, to find out what interests them and what they expect to get out of the meeting. Make sure you're prepared with all the evidence and materials you need to make your presentation as effective as possible.

Getting closer?

Preview the meeting *again* in your mind.

What's unclear? What looks unfinished?

Work out those details.

Preview again.

Make corrections.

Again!

This is the process. And the interesting thing about those mental repetitions is that every time you run them, the scope and details of the presentation actually become clearer. In other words, it's more than a mental exercise, because it has real-life impact and real-life results. When you finally stand up to deliver your presentation, you *are* better prepared. You *have* cleared up the details. All that mental work has a real payoff.

Plotting a Change of Course

A careful preview also helps you realize, early on, that you may have to set a new course or rethink the plan. Senator Wilson *knew* that his proposed amendment might be shot down by both Houses of Congress. So at the same time he was pressing for passage of the resolution, he was prepared to start off on a different tack—getting the states to call for a constitutional convention. When we met Michael Fay for the first time in court, I *knew* we might lose the case, and I was already thinking out a strategy for designing a boat and training a crew that would meet his challenge for the America's Cup. If you look ahead to the consequences of your present course—and they don't look good—the idea is to *tack now* so you arrive at your destination successfully:

• An athlete realizes that he has to change coaches and begin a new training schedule if he's going to be ready for the important trials next year.

• A manager finds out he'd better delegate a pet project that he's been doing on his own. (Otherwise, that project is going to hang around his neck forever, which is no good for the organization and not much good to the people he's supposed to be managing.)

• Someone who has every intention of being a good parent discovers that his social life has been getting more attention than his kids. Seeing what help the kids need—in the long view—

makcs it easy to decide what part of his social life can be given up.

• A busy professional working out her schedule for the coming year realizes that it's too jam-packed with activities—and a number of those activities are irrelevant to her goals. The preview helps her decide what committees she can give up and what meetings she doesn't *have* to attend.

When you preview future events, what do they look like? What happens when you "roll the cameras" and look at your upcoming days, weeks, or months? What do you see? Can you chart a clear course?

The ability to plan ahead for many contingencies—like the ability to do research—is the *action* part of a winning performance. Doing your homework gets you prepared to strategize. But a strategy that is inflexible, that doesn't allow for changes in conditions or tactics, is almost worse than no strategy at all. Whether you're in sailing, politics, or business, you have to be ready for that sudden change of course. And then prepare *thoroughly* so there are no surprises.

The rest is just hard work.

And the hard work begins when you *draw up your list and get in shape.*

9

Draw Up Your List and Get In Shape

Previewing the process helps you prepare for hard work, pressure, and action. But when you're in the *middle* of the action, how do you keep things organized? How do you keep your priorities straight? How do you keep track of thousands of details?

Draw Up Your List!

In March 1988, with the next America's Cup less than six months away, I had no boat, no crew, no agreement on a race site or a set of rules, and a lot of provisional endorsements from sponsors who wondered if the race would ever take place.

The New Zealanders had fought their way through the New York courts, where a judge allowed them to challenge us in a ninety-foot-waterline monohull. But Michael Fay had threatened to drop out of the race if we used a catamaran. When we stuck to our guns, he made moves to change the date and allow more entrants. When we said the date was fine with us, and we'd still see him in a catamaran, he began making noises about going to court again (which he subsequently did, on May 25, 1988).

So there we were, in March, preparing to sail the world's

premier match race in a boat that might or might not be allowed, against an opponent who might or might not show up (we had competitive reasons to believe he would), for a date that might or might not be agreed to (we had sent Michael Fay the race dates—he had not responded), under rules that had yet to be determined (Fay owed us a response on that one, too).

Such were the conditions on March 12, 1988, the day I stepped onto the springy trampoline of a Formula 40 catamaran for my first real day of practice. We didn't have another 40 to race against, but we had a strong challenger in Skip Banks from Norwalk, Connecticut, who was sailing a twenty-five-foot C-Class catamaran with a hard-wing rig. Crewing for him was John Marshall, who wanted some hands-on experience with the rig that his team was designing. (At that very moment, Scaled Composites was working away on the computer screen for *Stars & Stripes '88.*)

I'm not careful with boats. I like to see what they'll do. If something's going to snap, I want to find out today so we can fix it and it won't happen again tomorrow.

So we broke a few things on the 40. But it was a good day—and the start of a learning experience for me. I began to see how a cat performs—and there are a lot of differences between a multihull and a monohull. I also watched the "C" to compare the performance of the gull-wing. I wanted to see how Skip handled it, so I could try it out the next day.

We were out about six hours, and all the time we were out there—tacking, jibing, taking times, matching our speed against the "C"—I was ticking off things that needed to be done.

By the time we got back, I knew a lot more about catamarans and what they would and would not do.

But most importantly, I had started *the list.*

It was already in my head. Item after item. Check this, look into that, change the other. The list was about a mile long.

I didn't know whether the whole mess of the America's Cup challenge was going to be unscrambled by September '88, but by the time we came into the dock, I didn't have to worry about all that.

All I had to worry about was *the list.*
Everything on that list *would* get done.
As far as I was concerned, America's Cup '88 had begun.

Delegating Lists

The first list started at the dock while we were still tidying up. Different people on the team would handle different things:

- Someone has to fix the stuff that broke.
- We want to add ten feet to the mast for more sail and more speed. Find out how soon that can be done.
- The trampoline is too springy. We're bouncing all over the place. Run some lines under it and tighten them up so it's stiffer.
- There's kelp on the daggerboards and rudder. It's a lot of drag. Let's talk to John Marshall and figure out a way to keep that kelp off.
- I want the kind of wind indicators Skip has on his boat. See if he can make me one.

. . . And on . . . and on. . . .

At the Chart House Restaurant that night, I put everyone I needed to talk to near my end of the table. I had someone from the design team, someone from the crew, a couple of guys who knew more about multihulls than I did, and everyone who had been on the boats that day. We poured our wine, ordered our meal. Then I said the fateful words that everyone knew they would hear:

"Okay, let's start our lists."

Lists Make Performance

I live by lists.

I can remember most of the things on my lists, so I don't always write things down. But when I'm *assigning* things, I do expect other people to be writing—fast.

If you can't *remember* the things on your list, you *have* to write them down.

You can win races by lists.

You can run companies by lists.

Anyone who works with me or crews for me learns to respect those lists, or they don't work for me or crew for me anymore.

A list is a beautiful thing. Here are some things that a list can do for you:

It's a tracking system. When I go into a meeting with a list and run through the whole thing with my team, I don't throw it away or forget about it. I'm done with it for the moment, but they aren't. They have to put completion dates next to items on the list. If it's a long-range plan, they have to chart out some action on it. If something doesn't get finished, that list comes back to haunt them. Eventually, I'll go back to the list again, and I want to see everything checked off, or I'll find out why it wasn't done. However, a list also . . .

Clears the mind. Between the time I read out the list and the time I check up on it, I don't have to worry about it at all. Of course, things come up during the day, and I'll ask how someone's coming with this or that. But the point is, I don't *have* to worry about it, because it's all being enacted *and I'm not doing it.* That frees me up. I can worry about what's next while they're worrying about that stuff, and when we all get together and see where we are, we've all moved forward. If I had to circle around checking on people, we'd all move a lot slower, and I'd be one of those pain-in-the-neck types who hovers over everybody. This way, everyone's working on the list. And what that does is . . .

Generates sublists. When I say, "Add ten feet to the mast," naturally I have some preconception about how they might do that, but someone else has to deal with it. Someone has to figure out how to design the piece that's going to go on the top of the mast. Someone has to arrange to have a new sail cut. They have to go through the logistics of unstepping the mast, repositioning the shrouds, and getting it all together in time to take it out for another practice run. Somewhere, someone starts their own *sub-*

list to make that happen, but I don't have to worry about those details. The item on my list is *conceptual;* the items on their lists take care of the *execution.*

Get the Sequence Right

I'm not the first listmaker in history, of course. Practically everyone I meet who's successful in anything has their own, personalized list system, calendar system, date-keeping system, and scheduling system. If you have ever wondered how busy, overworked, high-profile people keep their priorities in order, the best clues are probably locked away in their system of day-to-day organization. The "person who does a thousand things at once" does not really do a thousand things at once (at least, if he or she is doing them well). What he actually does is one thousand things in very rapid sequence. The real talent, the real trick, is being so secure with your *sequence* of things that you can concentrate on the matter at hand—knowing that the next item on your list will pop up at the right time, and you'll be able to shift your attention to that.

Once you've made your list, trust it. If things come up during the day, jot them down. Don't attack them immediately, if you can possibly help it. Find that five minutes of contemplation somewhere when you can look over your jumble of problems and put them in sequence.

Who Can Help?

Of course, when you're in the middle of a complex operation or trying to solve a difficult problem, all the options, priorities, and possibilities don't occur to you in logical sequence. In fact, at the end of the day you may be looking at a pile of problems a mile high and wondering where to begin digging. Before you can think about getting things organized, you have to get it all out on the table.

That's when a good listener can be a valuable ally—especially if that listener can help you get organized. It could be a friend. Your spouse. A business colleague. In my case, during two America's Cup campaigns, the listener was Ed du Moulin.

The former vice chairman of Bache & Co. (now Prudential–Bache), Ed du Moulin is an accomplished sailor and a great friend who stood by me in the heat of the '83 and '87 campaigns. When I was sailing *Liberty* in the Cup defense at Newport in '83, and again in our '87 campaign (as a trustee), he made himself available as confidant, executive troubleshooter, and behind-the-scenes manager. Almost without a break, he was on hand to help me and the *Stars & Stripes* "gang" (as he calls them) in the long haul from '85 to '87.

While I was caught up in the daily pressures of training a crew, testing new designs and equipment and working on logistics, I counted on Ed to make sense of what was happening and help restore order. In the midst of troubles with clubs, committees, syndicates, sponsors, and the media, Ed provided balance. He listened to my gripes. He gave focus to the blur of events taking place.

I knew that, at the end of any day, I could barge in on Ed and his wife, Eleanor, whenever I had finished the one thousand and one things I had to do. It was a place where I could put my feet up—and Ed heard about everything that had gone wrong during the past twenty-four hours. I sometimes kept on talking until I had dumped all the problems in Ed's lap. He listened, asked my opinions, and, when necessary, let me ramble.

But he and I both knew it wasn't just rambling. Quietly, efficiently, always working behind the scenes, Ed was drawing up his list of things that needed to be done. He would go out the next day and begin fixing whatever was wrong. While I went out and stirred up a new nest of trouble, Ed patiently talked to people, found out what needed to be done, soothed whatever feathers had been ruffled, and made sure our campaign stayed on course. Though we hardly saw each other during each day, I always knew Ed was working on his list—and getting the campaign in shape.

Choose Your List—and Use It

There are different *kinds* of lists. People I've observed in sports and business tend to favor one kind or another, but some of them use all. Here are the categories I've identified:

• *The night-before list.* This is the list that Ed du Moulin helped me with. It's clean-up from the day just past and preparation for the day to come. Jot down everything that's a loose end, along with every new problem that cropped up during the day. Then think about tomorrow: what *must* be done and what *might* be done. Number everything, check off the things you can delegate, and make sure there's something on the plan for tomorrow that will really move you ahead. Then go to bed. (And, if you can't sleep, add to your list until your mind is cleared of all that junk and you *can* sleep.)

• *The morning list.* This has to be done before the phones start ringing. Lock the door. Write down the nastiest, worst tasks and problems first. Keep them first on your list, and get them out of the way as soon as possible. If you put off the nasty stuff, it'll poison your whole day.

• *The airplane list.* For some reason, being in transit from place to place—by car, by plane, by train—gives you a better perspective than just about anything else. Some of my most far-sighted, goal-oriented, long-range plans have been executed in list form on a plane somewhere eight miles above the ground.

• *The performance list.* Many coaches use this after a game to critique their players' performances—say, after they've shown a video of the quarterback getting hit from four sides as he's about to make a pass. I prefer to avoid the critical angle: if there's been a foul-up, we don't just pick out what went wrong, we run through what has to be done so it won't happen again. If we lost pressure in a jumper strut in the previous race, why beat on the guy who left the valves open and let it happen? Everyone knows what happened anyway. Instead, we're going to make up a checklist that ensures it never happens again. And it won't.

• *The laundry list.* All the items. All the details. Everything that needs to be shipped, packed, ordered, resupplied, forwarded, returned, and completed. For me, these are like the sublists, the ones I delegate to other people but look over from time to time. They're a good way to find out what the people on your team are *really* doing.

Make Your Next Memo a List

A list is part of your mental performance. It makes you go through the paces, act out the whole scenario. You have to decide what belongs there and what doesn't. You have to put things in order. If you don't get something done, it keeps showing up, moving around, and waving at you. Lists turn thoughts into actions—and keep you honest.

When you write your next memo, consider making it a *list.* Too often, memos are overwritten and light on content. There are the kinds of vague memos that tell someone you might decide to do something . . . but only if everyone agrees to have a meeting to decide whether it should actually be done. And then you send copies of the memo to everyone you want to impress, influence, remind, or take a shot at.

If your memo is a list, it doesn't do any of that. It's not a political instrument. It's an *action* instrument.

It tells you and the people you send it to which things *have* to be done if you want to get from point A to point B. And they *will* be done!

PART 3

Teamwork

10

Look for Hunger

Anyone who watched America's Cup '87 on TV got a good, close-up view of my crew working together on *Stars & Stripes*. Announcers on ESPN took note of the fact that the team worked together smoothly, without any yelling or rushing around. There were no fireworks on *Stars & Stripes*, but there wasn't any lack of spirit either. When we won, we celebrated. But until we crossed the finish line, we were all business—a *team* business.

So it's no wonder that whenever I speak to an audience that includes managers and businesspeople, someone's sure to ask me: "How did you choose that team?"

My answer: "I just had three requirements: attitude, attitude, and attitude."

Finding people with the right attitude *is the most important step in building a team.* You may have a great, winning attitude yourself (a requirement I discussed in Part 1), and you may be a very inspiring leader. But your own attitude, energy, and leadership can't drive the team all the time. The people that you select for your team—whether in business, sports, or any other kind of cooperative work—should be the people who *want* to be there, who *want* to do a great job.

People who have the basic skills can always learn to perform better. Employees who are promoted can usually learn how to do their new jobs—and do them well. A new person on a team can find out how to work with other members of the team. But in order to perform exceptionally, learn new jobs, and work smoothly with highly competitive teammates, you have to pick people with a *winning attitude*.

So how do you pick the right people?

Where do you begin?

And once you have them on your team, how do you challenge and motivate them to stick with you and reach greater levels of achievement?

Let's begin with the first question.

How Do You Pick the Right People?

Commodore Robert G. Stone, Jr., of the New York Yacht Club, chairman of the board and director of the giant Kirby Exploration Company, Inc., formerly chairman of the board of States Marine International and West India Shipping Company, has hired hundreds of men and women for jobs with international responsibilities in management, engineering, exploration, and finance. Among his other responsibilities, he holds directorships at Combustion Engineering, Inc., the Chubb Corporation, Corning Glass Works, Great Northern Nekoosa Corporation, Hamilton Oil Corporation, Scudder International Fund, Inc., and Tandem Computers, Incorporated—to name a few—where he has had a role in hiring many key executives.

I asked what he looks for in a prospective employee.

"They must have the guts and perseverance to stick at it when things go wrong. They have to maintain some humility along the way as they succeed, so their heads don't get ahead of themselves.

"But the most important thing is *hunger.*

"Is the guy *hungry?*

"I want him to say, *'Have I got the chance to be president of this company?'* and *'How long will it take me?'* "

Which Kind of Hunger?

For his own enterprise, Commodore Stone looks for people who are hungry for business success, advancement, corporate power, and financial rewards. For your own team, you may be looking for people who have a different *kind* of hunger. Here's what I mean by that:

- On *Stars & Stripes '87* I couldn't do anything with the guy who was motivated by money. At seventy-five bucks a week, he's not going to get rich.
- I couldn't help the guy who wanted a lot of job security. The job ended after eighteen months.
- I couldn't even promise fame. If we didn't win, none of us were going to be famous even for ten minutes.

But if he was motivated by the desire to sail with Dennis Conner, to get a good shot at winning the America's Cup, to learn a lot about sailing 12-meters, to work with a great team, and to have the opportunity to maximize his personal sailing ability, then he'd come to the right place. His motivations fit right in with what we were doing.

With those motivations *already in place,* he had a great attitude—and a *hunger* to succeed.

Now, what kind of hunger are you looking for in a team candidate? It all depends on the nature of the enterprise:

Is it high-risk? If so, you want people on your team who are hungry for risk and danger. If you're starting an entrepreneurial venture, be up-front about the risks involved. Let the candidate know that it's *not* a sure thing. Reveal what the percentages are as you see them. The person you want on your team will get charged-up, not discouraged, when he hears that there are great risks involved.

Do you want someone who sticks to the rules—or someone who shows a lot of independence? Some people are hungry for authority, discipline, the reassurance of having the top guy watch over them. They'll stick to the rules. Others like independence. They bridle under authority but flourish when someone gives them a lot of independence. Which kind of person are you after? *Respect the differences.* If you try to make the independent soul into a toe-the-line player, you're working *against* his personality. And if you hire a solid organization person for a high-risk job that requires initiative, you may be making a mistake.

Is there money in it? The fastest way to *de*motivate people is to fail to fulfill their hope for a fat salary or a big bonus. If there's real potential for financial gain in what you're doing, then by all means hire people who are motivated by money. They'll work, and work *hard.* But if the payout is going to be modest, don't go for the guy who is hungry for wealth. He'll lose interest as soon as he realizes that the rewards aren't what he thought they'd be.

Is there security in it? For some people, security itself is a great motivator. They can make a contribution to your team, but what they expect in return is that they'll still have a job next year or that you'll call on them again and again. Respect that. The hunger for security can be a great motivating force. Make the deal clear to them—"I'll give you all the security you need, but you have to be productive"—and you'll have a very loyal team player. On the other hand, you have to keep the bargain. If you take people who need security and put all kinds of uncertainties in their way, they rebel.

Is the work challenging? Constant challenge is more important to some people than money, job security, or steady promotion. For a position that requires daily repetition of the same task, with only small incremental improvements, you don't want the challenge-seeker. He's likely to become restless, and when he's restless he'll probably go looking for another team—or stir up trouble on yours. But give him a job that's "impossible," and he'll jump at the opportunity to prove he can do it.

Motivating someone who doesn't *want* to be motivated is the hardest work in the world. But if you find people whose motivations *fit in with what you're doing,* then you don't have to keep pushing them, reminding them, writing them memos, dreaming up incentives, or issuing veiled (and unveiled) threats. If they're already hungry when they come to you, all you have to do is feed that hunger.

People who give you resistance belong in another job—on another team. If you're faced with a difficult task, you're going to have a ton of resistance from other quarters. The one thing you don't need is resistance from your teammates. If you constantly have to motivate people to overcome their own inertia *and* overcome the outside resistance—that's pushing a snowball uphill. Your job becomes twice as tough.

So pick the person whose motivation fits the job!

Where Do You Find the Right People?

The teams in both *Stars & Stripes* campaigns, and the teams that work in my businesses, come from a wide range of backgrounds. Since *attitude* is the main qualifying criteria that I use, some of the more scientific methods of team-selection fall by the wayside. Of course I want someone with particular skills for a particular position. Beyond that, I don't conduct very methodical job-searches. *But I have my eyes open for good people all the time.*

And I think this is a critical point about looking for the right people for your team. Don't *over*look anyone. The right person could be sitting next to you on the airplane. He or she could be in your office. That person could be your best friend—or your most challenging competitor.

Specifically, here are some people to watch for:

· *Your friends.* My longest, most enduring business associates are Robert ("Scott") Scott and Barbara Scott. Scott Scott and I were fraternity brothers at San Diego State, and Scott married Barbara right after college. When he and Barbara got into the real estate business (after a stint at banking), we became partners in a real estate venture. That was about twenty years ago. I've been told that best friends don't make good business partners. Maybe this case is exceptional—all I know is that it's working fine. Great friends can be great teammates.

• *Your competitor.* Whenever I'm racing against someone who's outstanding—or I see someone on the crew of a competing boat who's exceptional—I try to find out more. To paraphrase the words of the outlaw Butch Cassidy in the movie that bears his name: Who *is* that guy? How long has he been sailing? Whom did he sail with, and where did he learn his stuff? I want to meet him at some point and find out what he has in mind for his future career. If I want him on my team and it seems as if he may be looking for a change, I'll let him know there might be a place for him. If he doesn't want to come over to my side right now, I'll at least start him thinking that he ought to *be* on my side.

Someone who is doing a great job for your competitor may not be totally happy where he is. In fact, he may be working to prove himself so hard because he wants to move up and out. An opportunity to work on *your* team may be just what he needs.

• *Your coworkers.* You can always pick the ones who are hungry. They don't complain. They see the stuff that needs to be done and do it without asking. They look for ways to complete their jobs faster. They share your motivations. They're on the lookout for new talent and new ideas. They suggest better ways to train or prepare, and they come up with ways to save money. They want to develop new products or bring more resources into the company. They never say anything's impossible. They put in more useful hours than the people around them, and they know how to get results by cooperating with other people in your organization.

• *People with blips in their backgrounds.* You're handicapping yourself if you select people who all have the same background and credentials. If you insist on screening your applications for people who have a lot of conventional education and training, what you may come up with, for a team, is plain vanilla.

But how do you mix it up? How do you find people who have different backgrounds and outlooks—who might suggest novel solutions?

Look for the blip in the background. Sometimes it appears on the résumé, sometimes you have to *ask* the guy or ask *about* him until you find out what's different. Suppose you're hiring an MBA who happens to be great at finance. He went to Yale, got a 3.8 average, graduated from Wharton, got a great job at Digital Equipment Corporation (DEC) . . . and then, suddenly, there's a blip on his résumé where he took a year off to cross the Kalahari desert by camel.

That blip tells you something. It indicates he has the guts to do something he really wants to do (attitude!) even if it jeopardizes the staight-line rise of his career. It shows he has the intestinal fortitude to face a hundred thousand square miles of desert by himself. It also indicates that he knows how to ride a camel across the desert—*and you never know when the skills of a camel driver* (or whatever) *might come in useful.*

The more blips you get in the background, the more likely you are to see a cross-fertilization of interesting ideas when you put these people together as a team. You'll get outcomes that would be impossible if everyone had similar professional backgrounds or were only trained in the same areas of expertise. Their blips give you greater power to be flexible and to meet the unforeseen.

Ask Around

When I'm considering looking at someone's potential for a job or team position, I always want to talk to people who have employed him, worked with him, or know his background. I ask a lot of questions—but always with a purpose. A thumbnail biography of someone can tell you worlds about that person's attitude.

For instance:

1. Suppose you are considering someone for a competitive team sport. You find out he always finishes first in local matches but when he gets to regionals or nationals, somehow he always ends up second or third.

ANALYSIS Obviously, he's got good skills, since he won all

those local matches. But the fact that he chokes when he gets to higher levels of competition says something about his attitude. As Robert Hopkins observed, when you get to a certain level, attitude becomes the determining factor in success. So you can assume that even though this person has the skills to win, he doesn't quite see himself as a winner.

The questions is, *why not?* Is he the kind of person who has huge amounts of talent, but just doesn't like to work very hard? Or does he just need a little push and guidance to get him over the top?

WHAT YOU HAVE TO DECIDE: Can I coach him to win at the higher level at which I want my team to compete?

2. You discover that the person you're considering for a job has held three jobs in the past two years. She's been promoted every time. All her recommendations are good. Now she wants to sign on with you, but she wants a significant promotion with an important new title and a big salary increase.

ANALYSIS: This is a hard worker who's ambitious and going places. But it's important to find out why she left each of those jobs and how she related to other people in those organizations. Don't *just* talk to the references she listed on her application. (She's a fast mover, so you can be sure she only listed people who would talk her up, and she may have given them a bit of coaching as well.) Try to talk to the guy who had the office next to hers or the business associate who had to travel with her.

What you have to find out is how loyal she's going to be. If she's moving quickly, it could be because she's only looking out for herself. Maybe she's one of those people who starts ambitious projects, gets a lot of headlines in the company, and then moves on before the hard work really begins—or before the actual results of those projects become known.

On the other hand, maybe she really is as good as she thinks she is, and she's just been underchallenged. The people who worked with her may give her a glowing recommendation, and add, "But she just wasn't happy here."

WHAT YOU HAVE TO DECIDE: If you keep her challenged, busy, and rewarded, will you have her loyalty to the team?

3. The person you want to hire is highly skilled—in fact, he has just the qualifications you want for the position you have to fill. But some of the people who worked with him before say that you have to keep him busy or he starts goofing off. He's never been fired from a job, but considering his ability, he hasn't risen as fast as he should have.

ANALYSIS: Is this a smart person who lacks drive, or someone with talent looking for a meaningful challenge? You may be able to find out a lot about his attitude during a one-on-one interview. Ask him what his goals are. If he gives a superficial, unsatisfying reply, you've got your answer: he either doesn't know what his goals are, or, perhaps, he has so little confidence in himself that he's afraid to talk about them. On the other hand, if he knows exactly what he wants to achieve, but says he feels underchallenged, this may be someone with a lot of potential.

WHAT YOU HAVE TO DECIDE: Since he doesn't seem to be a self-starter, you may have to keep throwing challenges in his direction. Are you prepared for the responsibility of keeping him busy?

Obviously, you can't tell everything about a person from a quick bio or even from an interview. But when you're looking for clues to *attitude,* look everywhere. If you intend to have that person on your team, in your office, or in your shop, it pays to ask a lot of questions beforehand.

Observe

No matter how good someone looks on paper or comes across in an interview, you can't really tell how he's going to work with you and the rest of the team until it starts to happen. There's always a shakedown period while you get to know each other. What do you look for during the trial period? What are the real clues to attitude?

1. Can he take a compliment? If you want to find out something about attitude, watch and listen carefully when you give the guy a compliment. Evaluation and criticism are universally difficult for anyone to take, but how a person takes a *compliment* is very revealing of attitude.

Does he take all the credit for himself and ramble on about what a great job he did? (If so, you've got a big ego to deal with.)

Does he belittle his accomplishment and say he really doesn't know how he managed to succeed? (That's an attitude problem of another kind: lousy self-image.)

Does he just say "Thanks" without adding any ego-inflation or making any apologies? (No attitude problem there.)

2. Does he repeat mistakes? Everyone on *Stars & Stripes '87* had a different range of skills and abilities. Some made more mistakes than others, especially at first. That was to be expected. I didn't mind when a guy made his first mistake. Someone would help him out, show him the right way to do it, and he'd have another chance. He might mess up a couple more times, but if he was paying attention and getting better, we knew he had a good attitude. Eventually he would develop the skills to do it right every time.

But when someone consistently made careless mistakes, we started to wonder. Does this guy really care? Is he paying attention?

You can show someone how to do something better. You can improve his game. But repeated mistakes are a reflection of not caring enough or not paying enough attention.

When someone on your team does work that is inconsistent and sloppy, you haven't got a training problem on your hands. You've got an attitude problem.

3. Does he help out? Watch him after he's finished his job, when everyone else is still working. Does he put his feet up? Or does he find out whether someone else can use a hand and help out the other guy?

If you have someone working for you who's hiding behind a job description ("It's not my job. I wasn't hired for that."), I suggest you tear up the job description. Otherwise, you'll never have a team. You'll just have a bureaucracy.

Attitude and Commitment

In our case, if winning the America's Cup was the most important thing in the world to a person ahead of anything else (education, career, hobbies, family), then he had the right attitude to make the commitment necessary to make the team and ultimately succeed. After the people on the team got to know me better, they joked that they should be *committed* for their "commitment to the commitment."

But when it was all over, every one of them was glad that he did make the commitment. They were the right people, with the right attitude, motivated in the right direction. With those qualities going for them, they *had* to make up a great team.

11

It Takes Commitment
to Qualify

Now that you've hired the candidate and made him a member of the team, you still have to find out: will he stay on the team? Will he show the kind of *commitment* it takes to qualify? In order to win, your teammates have to develop the same kind of commitment that *you* have. Of course, you can't read the minds of your employees or your crew, but there are ways to encourage and test for commitment.

Can He Keep Up the Pace?

Harold Geneen, the legendary head of ITT, was famous for long hours. When a venture was underway, he kept his executives after 5 P.M., often after 10:30 P.M., and sometimes after 4 A.M.! Top executives in the American side of the multinational corporation could expect to spend about one week a month in Europe. They had to be ready to go anywhere, at any time, to meet people, solve problems, review numbers, attend meetings, restructure companies. In his twenty years at ITT, Geneen turned a company with sales of $766 million and marginal profits into a $22 billion giant that had 58 consecutive quarters of at least 10 percent growth in earnings.

"He was accused of being hard-driving, impatient, and tough on his subordinates," one writer observed, "but the accusations came from men who had left the company because they could not, or chose not to, keep up the pace. Those closest to him observed that he had little patience with 'phonies' who, for one reason or another, chose to 'wing it' rather than do the work required of them. But he had 'unbelievable patience' with people who sincerely were trying hard to do their best."

By the time Geneen retired as head of ITT, the alumni of "Geneen University" (as it came to be called) had gone on to hold top positions in 130 American companies. All of them were employees who had *kept up the pace* when they were working with Hal Geneen.

Commitment—the Glue

Commitment is the glue that holds the team together. If you're a Harold Geneen trying to run a multinational company that employs 375,000 people, you need quite a few people around you who are willing to stay after five o'clock. If you're Roger Penske and you want your car to win next year's Indy 500, you want a team that's willing to test cars all winter and spring at tracks all over the country. If you're a Jack Kemp making your bid for the presidential nomination, you want people who are willing to drop everything, come to Iowa or New Hampshire and dedicate themselves round-the-clock—without a guarantee of success in the campaign.

Just to qualify for teams like that, it takes commitment.

And commitment means sacrifice. The people on your team may have to give up some things. They're probably not going to get home in time for the evening news. Their social life may suffer. They might not be spending as much time with their families as they'd like to.

These sacrifices are significant. Some of them hurt. I wish I knew a way that people could make a commitment to the team without making some personal sacrifices, but I don't know a way. And from what I've seen, heard, and read about the way other teams operate, I'm not sure there *is* a way. Everyone who makes a commitment also makes some tough choices, and I recognize that those choices are tougher for some than for others.

This is the area where leaders and organizations most often come in for criticism from outsiders. Coaches who demand commitment are accused of being autocratic. CEOs are accused of being slave drivers—or they're seen as workaholics who push their employees into being workaholics. In amateur sports, anyone who pushes a team hard is accused of being "too professional."

What do these outside appraisals mean?

For one thing, they demonstrate that people *outside* a team have a real problem understanding the dynamics of what goes on *inside* a team. Some outsiders saw Geneen as a slave driver, but many of the so-called slaves considered their years at ITT the most intense, challenging, and exciting experience of their lives.

The NASA people who were part of the Apollo II team that put a man on the moon may have looked and acted like workaholics at the time, but ask any of them now whether they regret their commitment to that program.

The team of people who gave up most of their social life and outside interests to focus on the *Stars & Stripes* efforts may have looked "too professional" for an amateur competition, but none of them regrets the experience we had in Hawaii and Australia— or the experience that we had in 1988, matching wits and speed against a wild-card contender.

And I'm talking about *the experience* here—not just the big win, but what you take away from the *journey*. For the people at ITT, their experience translated into a diploma from "Geneen University." The team working on Apollo II came away with the experience of taking that first big step for mankind. On *Stars & Stripes '87*, and again on *'88*, the crews reached a confidence level that could only be achieved through thousands of hours of team effort and constant practice.

How Do You Test for Commitment?

How do you know if people have the commitment to qualify?

1. Give them something to do that's not in the job description. The willingness to help out is not only a sign of great attitude, it's also a sign that they'll commit to the team effort. When the crew of *'87* arrived in Hawaii—in mid-1985—the first thing they had to do was sand the hull of the 12-meter that we tested against *Stars & Stripes.* That job required hours and hours of backbreaking work. But it had to be done—we *had* to get that boat ready. To fair the hull, the crew worked from five in the morning until ten at night—*just sanding.* They had come to Hawaii to sail 12-meters, but for the first two weeks they had jobs as glamorous as hod carriers. No one had told them this would be part of the job—but on the other hand, no one had said it *wouldn't* be. Those who put in their two weeks of sanding and still hung on got a chance to sail; those who didn't, went home.

Other tests:

• The publisher of a small, start-up venture—a how-to magazine—welcomed his advertising director and editorial staff into bare offices. There was a pile of lumber stacked in the corner, along with cans of paints and paintbrushes. Before anyone went to work on the magazine, they had to build their own desks, paint their own offices, and put up their own shelves. (The people who stuck it out made that magazine into a success.)

• The president of a computer services company asked her new accountant to oversee the telephone-sales operation for a couple of weeks. The accountant stuck it out—scheduling the part-time employees who came and went, tallying results, listening to complaints, dealing with telephone-service foul-ups. (Seeing the potential in telephone sales, the accountant later did more work in the department, turning it into the most profitable operation in the company.)

• The vice president of a PR agency hired an associate without hiring a secretary for him. The associate did secretarial work for the first six weeks while he was also learning the business. (As a result, he realized that most secretaries also had time to handle account responsibilities: he reorganized the office and improved the company's incentive program. Business in that firm has increased by one-third.)

   • In one paper company, every newly hired MBA has to spend three months making new-account sales calls. Needless to say, the company has a customer orientation that has made it highly successful. Of course, some MBAs quit after a few days or weeks of making sales calls. But under the leadership of the ones who stayed on—and worked closely with the sales team—company profits have steadily increased.

It may seem as if you're "wasting a resource" to start someone out in a job that they haven't been hired to do. But consider: if that person won't work at the hard, dull, boring stuff before he goes on to the glamorous challenges, is he really part of the team? Or will he always expect someone else to do the dirty work for him?

2. Let the team-members run the test. In most businesses, it's fairly easy for employees to get along with the boss. All they have to do is say, "Yes sir" or "Yes ma'am," and do everything they can to please their employer. But obedience doesn't necessarily qualify an employee (*or* a crew member) to be part of the team. One other way to find out whether someone can be part of the team is to *let the other guys on the team test him.*

On *Stars & Stripes '87* and *'88,* the crews took care of the final selection process. They were always willing to help out a guy a few times, but they would be hard on someone who wasn't paying attention or who wasn't working hard enough to support his end of the operation. Anyone who repeatedly showed up late, left early, or who didn't help with the after-hours work took a lot of grief. The guys really decided if someone was a Sunday-afternoon sailor who didn't belong on the team.

The trouble is, a non-team player can do a lot of damage to a team:

· When there's a problem, he may shift the blame from himself to someone else. And when that someone else is *unfairly* blamed, there's a ripple effect of resentment.

· He or she can cast doubt over the campaign. There's a fine line between troubleshooting and troublemaking, between problem solving and problem creating. The negative individual who talks doom-and-gloom all the time can be a poisonous influence on a team that's trying to pull together.

When non-team players show up in the office, you can usually separate them right away from the team players. Two stereotypes come to mind when I think of negative individuals:

· *Blamers*, who are quick to point the finger at someone else whenever anything goes wrong.

· *Doubters*, who shake their heads about how badly the company is being run, or what a rotten deal they're getting.

These individuals are not an asset to any team, and they don't last long on mine. I rarely have to fire them myself. The other guys do it for me. The blamers and doubters—if I happen to make the mistake of hiring them—get the signals early, and they submit their resignations promptly.

I gladly accept.

3. Watch them during the clutch plays. When Michael Fay challenged our right under the Deed of Gift to meet his challenge by racing a catamaran in '88, John Marshall spent three days and nights with the lawyers who were preparing the court brief in our defense. During those long hours, John and the lawyers never left the law offices, while they discussed the issues, debated various approaches, drafted and redrafted the brief in order to present their case before the New York State Supreme Court.

John Marshall isn't a lawyer. His background, as a matter of fact, is in biochemistry. In the *Stars & Stripes* campaigns, he has played numerous roles as designer and organizer.

So what's he doing in the offices of New York lawyers at three o'clock in the morning, working on a legal brief to defend our entry in the America's Cup race?

Simple: it was a clutch play—and John is always there for the clutch plays.

If you want to see how committed someone is to the team, watch how he performs during those plays. Does he insist on leaving the office at five o'clock, even if there's a report due the next morning? Does he understand the significance of important meetings or does he treat them like casual events? Does he know when he's needed—and just show up—or does he have to be forewarned?

The committed men and women are available at all hours, anywhere.

And they're *always* in the right position during the important plays.

For a Committed Team—a Committed Leader

There's a flip-side to the commitment that team members make to a leader, and that's the commitment he makes to them.

Jesse Philips, the founder and chairman of the board of Philips Industries in Dayton, Ohio, is a self-made multimillionaire who has the right kind of commitment to his team of employees.

With no personal or family funds, Jesse—through hard work, scholarships, and loans—graduated from Oberlin College, earned a Harvard MBA in 1939, and immediately went to work for a department store in Dayton, Ohio. After eighteen years, he ended up owning the store, which he eventually sold. This gave him enough money, so he retired. After one year of retirement, Philips was bored. He decided to return to work, part-time. Jesse bought Jalousies of Ohio, a small company that made windows and doors for mobile homes and recreational vehicles, and turned it into Philips Industries.

Thirty-one years after he founded the company—working seven days a week—Philips has watched Philips Industries grow to employ 10,000 people, with 52 manufacturing plants in 20 states. It is a Fortune-500 company, listed on the New York Stock Exchange, with annual sales of over $900 million.

"Expect to work hard," Jesse told one young man who asked about starting a company. "Expect to work much harder than you ever worked before—harder than you thought you *could* work. And be prepared to take all the guff that comes along—because there'll be plenty of it."

That's the deal every leader makes with his team. You work as hard as they do. You make a great commitment. You take the guff that comes along.

But you can't inject commitment into your team if you, as a leader, don't have it. And you can't expect their commitment to be any *greater* than yours.

Philips believes that it is the obligation of a leader to listen to his team—to get all the input he can. The door to his office is always open, he answers his own calls—calls are not screened. Nobody has ever been fired for speaking his own mind. Once a decision is made, however, every member of the team is expected to quit quibbling and to use his best effort to reach the finish line. But Philips also believes that a leader has the right to expect commitment *from* his team. When he found that a few of his employees were using drugs, he immediately instituted a companywide anti-drug program including pre-hiring tests, tests for cause, and a free rehabilitation program. (In fact, Philips became a pioneer in introducing a national anti-drug program in industry.)

As Jesse sees his role: "I have the responsibility to give my employees the opportunity to learn, to achieve, and to recognize their results. It's also my responsibility to see that they're rewarded better than normal, both materially and emotionally—so there's a high return for the individual performer who sticks with Philips Industries."

Above all, says Philips, "I will never ask them to do anything I wouldn't do. I would not expect them to do anything against their moral or ethical values. I want employees to treat their suppliers, their customers, and their coworkers just as *they* would expect to be treated."

As Jesse points out, a leader has two responsibilities to his team. On the one hand, you're setting the pace and leading by example, because the people in your organization are watching your moves all the time. But you're also the one who's giving them new challenges and exposing them to new experiences and new competition. So you're helping every individual do things he could never do before, to succeed in ways that he could not succeed on his own.

And when you can do that, every one on your team begins to break through the "good enough" barrier.

12

Break the "Good Enough" Barrier

If the people on your team have a great attitude and they've demonstrated commitment, then you've got the right people and the right team.

But they don't know how good they can be!

They may *think* they do. Each one may have a clear image of how he's performed in the past. He's confident he can at least duplicate that performance. In addition, he may have a very high opinion—in fact, an inflated opinion—of what he can do this year, this quarter, or this season. But who knows how good your team can really be? How far can you push them? What can they actually achieve?

The only way to find out is through performance. And the only way I know to constantly and consistently improve performance is by breaking the "good enough" barrier.

Where's the Barrier?

Every time you hear the words "good enough," you're up against the barrier. Here's how those words translate:

101

· "That's *good enough* for government work."

TRANSLATION: "We work for a sloppy government that doesn't control costs or care about productivity, so why try to work any harder?"

· "That's *good enough* for today."

TRANSLATION: "We just finished our eight hours of work and that's all we got done, but it's quitting time, so let's go home."

· "That's good enough *for now*."

TRANSLATION: "We've left a lot of questions unanswered and problems unsolved, but, sorry, we just can't do any better right now. We'll get around to those problems later if we can."

We hear "good enoughs" all the time, on many teams, in many lines of work. Whenever a number of people are assembled in one place working on something together, *someone* is likely to speak up and say, "That's good enough"—and the other people in the group are likely look at the clock, nod their heads, and put down their tools.

That's when cars start falling apart.

That's when government work gets into huge cost-overruns.

That's when customers begin getting shoddy service.

That's when students no longer learn.

That's when skilled people stop upgrading their skills.

And that's when races are lost.

Push Back the Barrier

Teams may become uncomfortable when you start pushing back the "good enough" barrier. You may hear someone say, "We can't do that." If everyone has decided that getting a report out in one week is good enough, they may look stunned if you say it has to be done in three days. If they agree they can't sail any more today, they may look incredulous when you tell them you're going to sail the course one more time. Each time you make a new demand, you're pushing back the "good enough" barrier a little farther.

Pushing back that barrier creates resistance. To the people on your team, it's high jeopardy, high risk. But when you're building a team, you have to keep pushing—a little bit every day, and a *lot* over a period of time—if you want to see those people realize their full potential.

Different Barriers

Bill Trenkle, tailer on *Stars & Stripes '87*, now a vice president of DC Sports, is a team player with a great attitude and unbelievable commitment who has broken every "good enough" barrier that stood in his way.

Bill started working with me in the fall of 1978 when he was still at the New York Maritime College at Ft. Schuyler. His first job was on board the tender, the boat that keeps sails and spare parts. During the campaign for America's Cup '80, he graduated to the second-team pitman on board *Enterprise*. I knew right then I wanted to keep him aboard—and keep him away from the competition—so I had him crewing on *Retaliation* in the annual regatta of the Southern Ocean Racing Conference and later as a professional hand on the ocean racer *Lobo*. In the meantime, he graduated from Ft. Schuyler as a marine engineer, so he had engineering skills we could use in building and rebuilding boats.

By the time we got to the '87 campaign, Bill was at the heart of the team. When I asked him, he could always tell me how someone was doing—and usually his evaluation was right on the mark. When we had to decide on a color for the hull of *Stars & Stripes*, Bill was there mixing paint. When we had to cut up the hull of *Spirit* in '85 to add a wing keel, Bill was in charge of the job.

I've pushed Bill, but the pushing has paid off. He's broken every kind of barrier:

Physically: He discovered he could do more than stow sails, hand out spare parts, and do maintenance. Though he didn't have extensive sailing background—and, therefore, the confidence that comes from being around sailboats all your life—he found out that he had the physical skills and stamina to compete with the best of 12-meter sailors. That discovery came with hours and hours of practice, repetitions, and experience.

Mentally: He made the jump from *being evaluated* to *evaluating.* At first, he was always being tested. Could he get the job done on the boat? Could he trim the jib properly? Could he make the team? But pushed farther, pushed beyond the next barrier, Bill became the guy who did the evaluating. From *measuring up,* he had gone to *doing the measuring.*

I'm not doing Bill Trenkle any favors. I keep raising the ante. I'm making it harder. I keep saying our team has to know more, perform better, extend our limits, and reach new goals. On the other hand, Bill is the right person to challenge. He thrives on it. He doesn't know the meaning of "good enough."

Crashing Through the Barriers

Every leader has his or her own style of managing, directing, and guiding people around barriers. But how do you help your team *crash through?*

Here are some suggestions:

1. GET THEM IN TROUBLE—AND OUT AGAIN

Ed du Moulin, who helped guide so much of our '83 and '87 campaigns through troubled waters, has a philosophy that he used with the young, eager managers whom he hired (and often mentored) during his years at Bache & Co. He told me, "I couldn't wait for them to get in trouble."

Eventually, he knew, the eager ones would overextend themselves, overcommit themselves—they would make a couple of enemies in the organization, or they would take one too many risks. But rather than warn them too early, Ed looked forward to the moment when they would realize they *were* in trouble. When they made that discovery, he was standing by to help.

If you want people to crash through the "good enough" barrier, you have to be willing to let them get in trouble. One way to do that is by giving them unfamiliar responsibilities. If someone feels comfortable writing reports but uneasy giving a verbal presentation—assign him to give a speech the next time you have a big meeting. Now he's in trouble. In fact, if he has high anxiety about public speaking, he may be downright scared, though he's probably afraid to admit it.

Then give him the chance to get *out* of trouble—by rehearsing his speech with you or with other members of your team, or by assigning him to give short talks in front of an audience. You can guide him to other resources as well—speaking coaches, books, courses. When he's in trouble, he'll look for all the help he can get. But after he's crashed through, and succeeded, you'll have someone who can deliver a first-class presentation. You've just added a great asset to your team without adding any new players.

2. BE CONSISTENT

Charles Garfield, who worked on the Apollo II NASA program, went on to study the personalities of people in business, science, and education whom he saw as "peak performers." One of the most significant personality traits of peak performers, he noted, was *consistency:*

> Peak performers are people who approach any set of circumstances with the attitude that they can get it to turn out the way they want it to. Not once in a while. Regularly. They can count on themselves.

As a leader, you have to be able to count on yourself to produce results. Not once or twice, but again and again.

Being consistent with your team is critical. What's the point of asking someone to complete their job in five days if you don't ask for it five days later? People learn you *mean* it. If your actions tell them that *you don't follow through,* they will quickly discover that *they don't have to follow through either.*

3. RECOGNIZE TEAM PROGRESS

Team progress is different from individual progress—and the reward system differs accordingly. Bill Trenkle observed, "When Dennis is happy, he talks about it." I sure do. I say, "We were faster on that leg." Or: "I like this new jib."

I'm not complimenting anyone directly, because I wouldn't know whom to compliment. Me? I didn't make that new jib. The other guys in the cockpit? They're not responsible for the improved jib. The sailmaker? He did a great job, but all the same, someone had to pay for it; someone else ordered it; and someone important worked the machine that stitched it together. And if the crew hadn't hoisted it right, trimmed it right, and spent six hours and eighty-five tacks testing it, we never would have *known* it was a better sail.

Rewarding individual progress may give some guy an ego boost—and I'll do that if he has taken a personal risk or done something really astounding. But the best way to reward your team, as a team, is to be happy when you make progress. Talk about it:

- If a new office setup is working well, tell everyone how much you like it.
- If your company just signed a big contract, let everyone know this contract is going to keep all of you prosperous and happily employed.
- If you just got a decision in your favor, or you succeeded in meeting an impossible deadline, talk about how well things went.
- If your team reached a new productivity goal, put the new record up on the chalkboard and let everyone see it there.

It's the *whole team* that breaks the "good enough" barrier together. No matter how great each person is, *he didn't do it alone.* Mark the team's progress—but let each person draw down his own dividend.

4. BE THE BOSS

Why pretend you're not? You make the decisions. You take the guff. If your team loses, it's you who is on the line.

I don't go for the skipper or boss or coach or entrepreneur or politician who wants to be one of the boys. Why pretend? You're the guy who might have to drop somebody from the team, fire an employee. You're the person on whom the decision finally rests.

John Madden, who coached the Oakland Raiders to winning the Super Bowl in 1976, the first coach to lead a single team to more than 100 victories in either the NFL or AFL, may seem like the guy-next-door as a sports announcer. But as a coach, he never was.

These are his words:

> Too many coaches want to be "one of the guys" but that's the worst thing a coach can be. Your players don't need another friend. Your players have all the friends they need. Sometimes too many. Your players need someone to tell them what to do. Your players need a coach, a teacher—not a friend.

Right.

You can get a show of hands, measure your yeas and nays, but ultimately you decide what play the team is going to make. It's a major mistake to pretend (a) You don't have the power to make those decisions; or (b) You aren't really responsible for the decisions you make. That's commonly called "passing the buck."

At the same time, I would never downplay the friendships that develop through working together. In business and in sailing, I've made friends who will last me a lifetime. Sometimes it's all inter-twined—the business, the team effort, the shared interests, the common goals. In some areas, *they're* the boss—and I know that. But when it's my turn to be boss, I *take* my turn. I'm not one of the guys anymore. They know it; and so do I.

5. MATCH WITS

One of the best ways to crash through barriers is by bringing together the most challenging minds—and letting them challenge each other. In the '88 Cup effort we brought together Dick Rutan, designer of the Voyager airplane, with six designers, six technical consultants, three sailing consultants, and two meteorologists—all under the leadership of John Marshall, the design project manager. Each member of the team had a different idea about how the boat could be built. It was a matching of wits that produced the solution.

In almost any company, matching the wits of the best people on your team can push everyone beyond the "good enough" barrier. If the people in operations always have their own meetings, they may begin talking and thinking in one language—operations. The next time there's a meeting, why not get someone from sales or marketing to join them? Why not someone from personnel? Why not an office planner? Often, the most interesting developments come about because of challenges from outside. (Many managers know this, yet typically exclude people from outside their own departments.) If you've *hired* people with blips in their backgrounds (see page 86), this is a chance to include them in the matching of wits—and help *everyone* crash through those barriers.

6. LET THEM KNOW IT'LL NEVER END

Henry Childers, a grinder on *Stars & Stripes '87*, had never sailed on a 12-meter before he joined the team. Though he agreed to give it a try, he hadn't expected the welcome he got in Hawaii. He arrived on a Friday night and by ten o'clock Monday morning he was in his first practice race—in foul weather and a thirty-knot breeze.

Henry soon got used to long days—very long days—in the boat. In Hawaii we were usually out sailing by ten o'clock—but sometimes we weren't. We made it back before dark—except for the times we didn't make it back before dark. Everyone had one day off a week—except when we couldn't take a day off. We got to bed early every night—except the nights we never got to bed.

As Henry Childers says, "We didn't waste our energy wondering when it was going to be over."

As far as I'm concerned, worrying about when it's going to be over *is* wasted energy. The team that starts to focus on when's-it-going-to-end, when's-my-time-off, and when-can-I-get-away is losing track of what it has to accomplish.

The clock kept running. Every hour, we were one hour closer to Australia.

How do I know at the beginning of the day whether we'll need an extra hour—or five hours—to test a sail, finish a report, or close a deal? How can anyone encourage commitment, creativity, involvement, dedication, and then announce, "Okay, it's five o'clock—you can turn off the lights and go home!"

Stop the Clock-Watching

Projects have an end. Goals are met. Races begin on time. But the process of working on projects, meeting goals, and preparing for races is continuous and unending. If you have employees who are more concerned about having dinner on time than about completing a project, they should be in the fast-food business.

Clock-watching is not productive. It doesn't get the results you want. It doesn't leave room for human error, fallibility, and normal foul-ups.

Let your team get the job done, then look up and see what time it is.

When people find out that's how you operate, they don't waste energy wondering when it's going to be over.

Instead, they keep their heads in the game.

13

Keep Their Heads in the Game

Everyone who works with me knows I ask a lot of questions, but even those who have worked with me the longest don't know when new questions may come up. I don't send out a memo proposing a new idea and ask everyone to think about it and report to me at the next meeting. Instead, I might stop someone in his office and ask something like:

> "Why can't we start a new line of licensed products in Japan? Do you know any sports company that's done that? How successful were they? How long would it take us to get it going? Who do we need to talk to? What's stopping us?"

Or I might catch a guy as he's about to leave the office. Suppose there's a deal that's been hanging for several months:

> "Can we close that deal this week? Well, what if we make them a final offer? What will they do about that? What if we tell them we're going to walk away?"

When we launched *Stars & Stripes '88*, there was a lot of work to be done on the wing on the catamaran. But every additional day that we spent fixing it meant another day lost from practice before the race. So I asked:

"Why can't we get that done by tomorrow morning? How many people will you need? Who are they? Do we have the parts? Can you get them this afternoon? Do we need to fly in anyone to work on it? How soon can they come?"

When we put up a new building in San Diego for Dennis Conner Sports and Dennis Conner Interiors, I walked around the site with the contractor and asked:

"Can we put a window here? Does the shop have enough light? Can we get this done by next Tuesday? Do we have enough parking places? Where will the loading guy back in his truck? Who's going to lease the extra space? Where's the runoff from the driveway going to go? Can we get the landscaping done by Thursday?"

Leading Questions

The purpose of all these leading questions is to challenge assumptions, pose alternatives, or suggest a new course of action. They are the kinds of questions that *keep people's heads in the game.*

Questions like that demand a thoughtful response. Maybe the person who's negotiating the deal for us thinks it's impossible to finish up the negotiations this week. At least the question gets him thinking about it. I'm not demanding that it be done. I'm wondering, "What if . . ." and suggesting another possible tactic or an innovation. But when you put it that way—as a possibility— you get *other* people thinking about the possibilities.

I got into this habit of asking questions of my crew early in my racing career. It works with a crew, and it works just as well with business associates, experts, consultants, and even clients and sponsors. For me, asking questions is the first step toward delegating decision making. Before you can hand over decisions to people, you have to be sure that their heads *are* in the game. You want them to be thinking about different moves and considering alternatives *even when you're not around.* Ask lots of questions, and they'll get into the habit of asking themselves: *Can this be done?*

Discuss the Problem

Too many head guys believe that they're supposed to have all the answers. The way I look at it, that's impossible. Whether you're in business, sports, or any other field, it's impossible for you to have all the information, all the strategies, tactics, and know-how to win the game.

On the other hand, a problem won't go away if everyone ignores it. Talk about it. Bring it up every morning, if necessary: "Does anyone have any ideas about this . . . ?" Charge into somebody's office: "What's our strategy for . . . ?" Take people aside: "You know, this information we received. What do you think . . . ?"

If you bring the subject up once and never mention it again, everyone will think you've taken care of it—*even if the problem still persists in front of their noses.*

If you bring it up twice, they'll begin to think you're serious about finding a solution.

If you keep bringing it up again and again, asking for your team's opinion, asking what different people are going to do about it, they'll realize it isn't just *your* problem. It's *everybody's* problem. And they'd better work together to do something about it.

Suggest the Impossible

"Brainstorming" has become such a polite process in most businesses that it has lost its most potent power—the shock value. A real brainstorm should be just that—a full-scale, seventy-knot mind-bender, complete with thunder and lightning. You lose the shock value if you politely call a meeting, seat everyone around a table, make sure they all have cups of coffee in front of them, and say, "Let's have a brainstorming session. Who wants to go first?"

That's not storming; that's wheedling.

Preserve the shock of surprise. Catch your people when they're *not* at a meeting, when they *haven't* been alerted by a memo— and pop the questions. You'll quickly find out whether their heads are in the game.

Create Competition

Dollar bets are just one way to create competition. Other methods work, too. If you have put together a team that likes to compete, why shouldn't they compete with each other—within reason?

Inside some companies that do technical research, competing groups are set up to find multiple solutions to the same problem— the famous "performance shootouts" that help keep monster companies creative. Hewlett-Packard (HP) has a competitive system whereby each division has to sell its new product to the sales force. Unless the HP group that developed the product gets acceptance from its own sales team, the division's product won't make it to market.

If inside competition is held at a reasonable level, it's a healthy injection for your team.

The whole *Stars & Stripes '87* campaign was built on the fiercest and fairest internal competition we could arrange—two well-matched teams on competitive boats crewed by committed people with almost equal skills, battling it out on the water every day. The competition was controlled by environment: the two teams ate together, worked together, and shared the same dorm. There was no enmity—just *competition*—and that competition kept a campaign alive through the eighteen months when we never raced against any outside team.

Here are some other tactics you can use with your team to keep their heads in the game.

1. REVIEW THE PLAY

John Madden recalls the first time he went to a coaches' clinic given by Vince Lombardi. The subject of the clinic was "The Green Bay Sweep," a play run by Paul Hornung with Jim Taylor and two guards. Madden thought the talk would be short and sweet. "After all," he wondered, "how long could even Vince Lombardi talk about one play?"

The answer was *about eight hours long*—four in the morning, four in the afternoon, with a break for lunch. Vince Lombardi, Madden recalls, "stood up there at the blackboard with a piece of chalk and dissected the Green Bay sweep player-by-player— each player's assignment against every possible defense, against every possible stunt, against every possible blitz, against every possible coverage."

In any game where there are patterns of plays, a team can fall into the habit of doing the same thing in the same way every time. They turn into an excellent machine. But if you want that machine to be ready for emergencies, prepared to take the initiative, and shift their tactics at a moment's notice, they have to review their plays.

Any coach who replays the video of a game will stop the tape at certain points and ask, "What happened there? What could we have done differently? How can we take advantage of that situation next time?"

Anyone who manages other people in a business situation can "stop the tape" in another way—by reviewing a transaction that just took place:

• *After a negotiation,* review the strategy you used and the strategies used by the party on the other side of the table. Ask your team: "What were our most effective tactics? What would we do differently next time? How well did we anticipate their moves? Did we find out anything that we should apply to our next negotiation?"

• *After a sales call,* it always pays to review exactly what happened and what next steps must be taken to close the sale.

Often, promises or suggestions that were made during the meeting will require some follow-through. Who (on your team) is going to take care of that? Do each of the people on your team know what their responsibilities are? Do they know *when* things are supposed to happen? If you want your customers or clients to be satisfied, your follow-through has to be just as thorough as your sales call.

   • *After a presentation,* hold a debriefing with everyone who was involved. In *their* opinion, how did the meeting go? Was it effective? What kind of feedback did they get from the people who were there? What were the high points of the presentation? Where did it sag? What's your game plan for your next meeting?

   It's easy to review the play when everything went well—not so easy when things went badly. People may want to point the finger. A lot of blaming can go on. It's important to use your questions to keep the review on target. Focus on what can be done better or differently *next time,* to avoid mistakes and get the success you're looking for.

2. RESTATE THE TEAM'S PURPOSE

In large organizations, *the purpose of the game* can get lost among a lot of side issues and distractions. In fact, the larger the organization, the harder it is to keep everyone's head in the same game. That's why you may have to keep bringing them back to the purpose of working together as a team. You may have to remind them of your *common goal.*

   The employee who has been locked into the same job for many years may believe that his purpose is to get through the week, collect a paycheck, take as much time off as possible, and accrue benefits. You might have to remind him that his real purpose is to:

   • Make use of his skills, resources, education, and abilities to make a contribution to the organization.
   • Work with other people to produce results.

- Make the company more profitable.
- Introduce innovations or open new markets.
- Get things running more smoothly.

In a big company these purposes can get lost. The immediate goals—the next paycheck, the day off, the bonus—are much more visible than the long-term goals of making the company more innovative, productive, or profitable. Sometimes, team players lose sight of the common goals of the organization because *no one reminds them.*

A question can be a reminder:

"Can you think of a way we can do this better?"
"Have we compared costs?"
"How about working with _____ on this project?"
"Is there another way to get results that we
  haven't yet considered?"

Of course, there's more to it than just asking questions. You have to listen to the answers and let your employees know that their suggestions are being taken seriously. You have to assure them that they'll have access to the resources they need to put their suggestions into action. If someone's suggestions on how to cut costs or do a better job are ignored, they quickly lose interest in the game. They'll stop thinking about the problem. The Question-and-Answer will be an exercise and nothing more.

3. SELL YOUR TEAM ON SELLING

Mark H. McCormack, the outspoken, charismatic head of International Management Group, is a master salesman. In the late fifties Mark began negotiating contracts for Arnold Palmer—since then, Mark has turned IMG into a multimillion-dollar multinational corporation that manages the careers and investments of hundreds of celebrities and sports figures. IMG is an intensely competitive organization, and everyone who works for McCormack quickly discovers that he and his organization demand total commitment.

IMG has a great team, and Mark is a master at *keeping their heads in the game*. He does it by selling from the outside in, and the inside out.

"Learn to sell," McCormack tells his people. "Realize that every interaction, whether it's baldly commercial or intimately personal, is in essence a selling situation.

"Young people, whether they know it or not, are born salespeople," he observes. "Getting peers to respect them, parents to trust them with the car, colleges to accept them—all that is selling. Everyone has those instincts. Don't start distrusting them when you venture into the business world."

As McCormack points out, everyone has to sell—a coach to his players, a quarterback to the other members of his team, a manager to his subordinates, the heads of a family to everyone else in the family. You're selling ideas, inspiration, cooperation, or a way of doing things. The people who report to you are your team and if they're going to be effective on your behalf, you've got to sell them on what you're doing in order to keep their heads in the game.

At IMG, where the product is service to clients, Mark reminds everyone in the organization that their business is *representing those clients*. Every client contact must represent the company's best performance. Whether an employee of IMG is answering a phone call, writing a letter, dealing with the media, visiting a celebrity, or talking to a potential sponsor, that employee is selling the image and performance of his company.

How does Mark McCormack keep their heads in the game? He sells the image and performance of IMG *to his own people*. When he meets with employees, he focuses their attention on the company's goals. When he writes a letter, holds a meeting, or talks to someone on his team, he is *selling* the idea that "We are IMG and this is the way we do business." As a result, everyone who works for IMG or deals with IMG knows what the company represents.

Whenever you're managing people, you have to sell them on your ideas and your way of doing things if you want to keep their heads in the game. Even if your company produces a tangible product, the service and attention that go along with that product are not created by machines and materials. Those "intangibles" are produced by the people who work on your team, who deal with your customers, clients, or sponsors. *They* have to keep selling; and *you* have to sell them on the idea of selling.

4. CREATE INCENTIVES

Incentives can *help* motivate the people on your team, but they can't do it all. Carefully consider the incentive program before you present it to your people. Which direction do the incentives take people? Do the incentives encourage people to undercut each other's performance—or to work together as a team? Do the incentives improve the whole company—or do they put star players in the limelight and give them disproportionate fame and glory?

Paul Hawken, the founder of the highly successful California tool company, Smith & Hawken, believes in shared ownership among employees—and he uses profit-sharing as an incentive. This produces a number of results that he's looking for. His employees are very conscious of customer relations, because they know that happy customers mean more business for the company. When problems arise, Smith & Hawken employees try to solve them as quickly as possible, rather than letting them sit on the desk, or passing those problems along to someone else. If customers get good service, if the company runs well, all the employees of Smith & Hawken benefit by sharing in the profits.

In some larger companies, there are cash awards to employees who suggest money-saving ideas to management. Those awards are built-in incentives for each employee to think about how his or her job can be done better or more efficiently.

Winning itself is an incentive—and everyone benefits if they get some of the rewards of being on a winning team. For the *Stars & Stripes* team, winning the America's Cup was a huge incentive—it had to be, since the financial incentives were almost nonexistent. Since that Cup represented the pinnacle of sailing achievement to everyone on the crew, it was worth working for. But when the moment of victory came, the whole team was sharing in that victory.

So the incentives have to be appropriate to the goals of the team; they have to be available to everyone on the team; and they must be incentives that push forward to the total effort. When they satisfy those criteria, incentives are an effective way to keep everyone's head in the game.

You're the Example

Once again, the leader sets the example. The eyes of your team are on you. If your head *isn't* in the game—if you are distracted by administrative trivia, personality conflicts, or office politics— your team is likely to be distracted rather than motivated by *your* activities.

I have seen managers become obsessed with details that should have been minor—and as a result, the whole team gets caught up in office politics. An office move, for example. A senior executive may become involved in deciding all the technical details of choosing people's offices, selecting the furniture, even deciding on design and layout. His involvement sends a message to everyone else in the office, something like: "This is the most important order of the day."

Soon there's whispering about where people are being moved, who gets the inside office, the outside office, the office with the biggest windows, and so on. A team that should be working together to produce results for the company is pulled apart—for a time—by rivalries over turf and uncertainties about position and prestige. And all because the guy on top got too involved. Rather than making the important decisions, getting people settled in, and getting on with business, he allowed the situation to become politicized.

If something is peripheral to the team effort, make your decision about it and get on with business. That way, the people who *want* to be on your team will keep their heads in the game.

It's Your Job

Keeping their heads in the game is *your work.* If you're a manager, that's what you do for a living. And it's hard work. It's an educating process. It's a growing process. You have to *keep asking,* even when you feel like answering the questions yourself, and you have to *keep listening* even when you think you know all the answers.

But this kind of work has an incredibly high payoff. As people like Mike Dingman, Fritz Jewett, Ed du Moulin, Hal Geneen, Jesse Philips, Robert Stone, and Mark McCormack have proven, *keeping their heads in the game* gives you a return-on-investment somewhere in the neighborhood of infinity to 1.

Just as important as the dollar return, when you keep their heads in the game, you also have the opportunity to cash in on your investment of time, energy, attention, trust, and commitment. That payoff—the biggest of all—comes along when you can *delegate decision making.*

14

Delegate Decision Making

Delegating decision making *could* be the most difficult thing you ever have to do. It's different from delegating some small task or giving someone a small area of responsibility. That's not delegating—it's bossing. When you're the boss, you can just say "Sweep the floors, clean the desks, and have the place locked up by nine o'clock." And it will probably get done.

But delegating *decisions* is different—and more difficult. It's more like, "Decide how you want to clean the floors and desks, set a time frame for accomplishing that task, tell me how many people you'll need do the job right, order the supplies, and set up a contingency plan in case one of your people doesn't show up."

The trouble with being a boss is that you *always* have to tell people when to sweep the floors. You become an order-giver rather than an administrator, a manager, or a leader. But what happens when you're not around to give orders? People don't know what to do. So they're likely to lean on their brooms and wait for you to come back.

If you can delegate the whole floor-sweeping operation, you're not just delegating the job, you're delegating the whole process of making decisions. The first step, of course, is to make sure they keep their heads in the game. But the second step is delegation—helping them figure out ways to do the job better, faster, or more efficiently.

People don't grow if they're doing their jobs without the power to change their jobs or their environment. In fact, management studies show that when people aren't allowed to make choices, they become progressively less productive. Having the *power* to make decisions—*whether that power is exercised or not!*—makes people more efficient and more productive. It's a big win for them.

It's also a big win for *you*. Every time you get a group of people who can carry out a plan without your making decisions and deciding every play, you increase your management power. Decisions can be made in your absence. Business can move forward while you're out of the office. Problems can be solved by others, instead of ending up on your desk. You can spend more time setting new goals and policy, and less time chasing after people to see if they've finished what they were supposed to do.

Send Them to the Foredeck

What if you now have a team that relies on you to make all the decisions? How do you get them accustomed to decision making?

One way is to send them up to the foredeck.

While he was an executive at Bache & Co., Ed du Moulin was also doing a lot of racing in his S&S-designed Pilot 33, *Lady Del.* He won more than fifty trophies, including the 1964 DeCoursey Fales Trophy (the Long Island Sound distance-racing award). With the crew on board *Lady Del* he used a management style that typifies the way Ed ran his business. If there was a disagreement about strategy between two crew members, Ed asked them to go forward to the foredeck, away from him, discuss it between themselves, and come back with an answer. When they agreed on a single strategy, Ed would follow it.

Being stuck behind the helm of a racing boat is probably the best training in the world for delegating decisions. Sometimes you can tell people what to do, but at the really critical moments, you don't have time. Each crew member has to be prepared to make his own decisions.

If the snap shackle fails on a spinnaker—as it did on *Stars & Stripes* when we sailed against New Zealand in the 1987 America's Cup semifinals—the decision to *act* has to be instantaneous. I could write up a whole manual of instructions for a crew faced with that contingency and it would be meaningless. Too many decisions have to be made too fast by too many people. The people on your team have to get used to working with each other instead of looking to you for instructions.

The next time there's a problem to be solved, a crisis to be met, or an operational decision to be made, you might consider a strategy for getting people on the foredeck. Gather the team in your office. Get the discussion going. Tell everyone you have to get to another meeting—you'll be back in half an hour. Then leave the room!

When you come back, ask for a report. What were the points of view? What did they decide? What course of action do they recommend?

If they spent that half hour talking about last Sunday's game, you've got some work to do. They may know how to fix that snap shackle, but they're not working together to *get it fixed.* Try the foredeck maneuver again . . . soon. Be explicit about your expectations: "I'm going to be back in half an hour, and I want your recommendations." Then let them make some decisions while you're out of the room.

Curbing Your Impulses

Of course, if you've had more experience than anyone else on your team, and you think you already know the way to solve all the problems, your impulse is to jump in and do it yourself.

Curb that impulse! Whenever you solve a problem, you're sending a message to the other people on your team that says, "I'll bail you out. I'll look after you. Don't worry too much about what's going on."

Wrong message. No matter how painful it may be for you at first, you have to let the other people on your team take the initiative in making decisions. Will they make mistakes? Yes, inevitably. But some mistakes are necessary if they're going to learn. It's the only way they'll see the actual results of their decisions.

In a small company that's having start-up pains, there's usually one person (the owner) who's trying to make all the decisions in the company. Because he invented the product or launched the company, the head guy thinks he has all the answers. He feels responsible for manufacturing, operations, management, advertising, sales, marketing, and customer service. It may take a long time for the owner to recognize that his specialty is primarily in one area, and that he needs support in other areas. For example, if his strength is in sales and marketing, then he needs someone else who can make key decisions about production and operations. Conversely, if the inventor is primarily a product-and-manufacturing guy, then what he really needs is someone who can make decisions about sales and marketing.

Many tales have been told of entrepreneurs who were unable to make the switch from *doing* to *managing* when their companies grew from small-and-simple to big-and-complex. The energy and skills of an entrepreneur often don't transfer well to the management of a larger organization. Knowing how to make all the critical decisions, the entrepreneur comes to believe that all the decisions affecting his company *can* or *should* be made by him alone.

Of course, the more people you hire and manage, the more you have to delegate decision making. Eventually, no matter how brilliant you are, you need to get other people to assist you by giving their advice or expertise. Also, the more decisions you can delegate, the more you can diversify.

I know something about real estate, but my success in the real estate business doesn't come from me: it comes from my partners, the experts, Scott and Barbara Scott.

I know something about boat design, but John Marshall and his team build better boats than I ever could.

I know what I want an on-board computer to do for me, but a smart guy like my navigator Peter Isler will have to evaluate what models are available and tell me which one we should be using.

I know something about making a piece of fabric into a drape and I know a lot about the interiors business in general, but I'll trust the manager of Dennis Conner Interiors to run the shop in my absence.

I look at it this way: I've worked hard to surround myself with people who know more than I do. I've put time and energy into building a team that knows what Dennis Conner wants to do. So why shouldn't the people on that team *make decisions that need to be made?*

Delegate Deal Making, Too

At Dennis Conner Sports we often do as many deals in a month as some companies do in an entire year. But while those deals are being initiated, negotiated, and finalized, I'm often somewhere else in the world, speaking, sailing, checking up on design developments, or meeting with a potential sponsor. Even when I'm in San Diego, I'm likely to be in meetings outside of the office, or out sailing.

If I had to closely monitor every deal throughout the negotiation process, Dennis Conner Sports would almost come to a standstill. So, as much as possible, I delegate deal making. In a typical situation, I have a meeting with Doug Augustine, head of operations. Suppose he has been approached by a company that wants to produce a "Dennis Conner" line of boats. Doug and I go over the proposal and come up with the five points we would like to present to the sponsor. For instance:

1. We want the logo to be a certain size.
2. We want to be able to approve the type of boat that's going to carry the logo.

3. We discuss what kind of up-front money we'd like to see.
4. We decide on a royalty.
5. And we decide how long the contract should run.

Then I go sailing, catch a plane, or look after other business. I'm out of the deal-making loop for awhile. In my absence, Doug has unlimited authority to negotiate the contract up to the point of making a final decision:

· If the boatmaker comes back and says the logo has to be smaller, Doug has to decide whether that's a deal-breaker.

· If the boatmaker changes his mind about what kind of boat he's going to produce, Doug has to decide whether the up-front money should be greater, whether the royalty should increase, and whether the contract should run longer.

· Does the boatmaker want our deal with him to be an exclusive? Doug will decide whether we should continue to discuss a contract.

· Is the boatmaker beginning to get cold feet about the price we're asking? Doug will decide whether to come down, hold the line, or trade off other options.

· Is the paperwork taking forever? Doug will turn up the heat.

· Is the other party being stubborn? Doug may make the executive decision to turn himself into a Royal, Number One, Pain-in-the-Ass.

Meanwhile, I'm in New York talking to PepsiCo, or in France at Perrier, or doing speeches, or looking at design plans, or sailing boats. But while I'm away, I'm confident that:

· The deal's moving forward. Maybe Doug's handling it himself. Or we may have delegated it to Dave McGuigan, my VP of sports marketing, or Dana Smith, VP for marketing. But *whoever has the ball is carrying it.*

· Points are being negotiated the way I would negotiate them if I were there.

· We have a good chance of closing, which is our overall

objective. The more deals we close, the more prosperous our business.

And, above all . . .

• If there's an issue that might be a deal-breaker, Doug will bring it to my attention. He'll have the facts together—and they'll be accurate. He'll be able to explain the problem in two hundred words or less. And he'll be able to recommend at least one alternative course of action.

If there's a hitch somewhere, we can review the problem, decide whether to walk away or move forward. I might have to make one phone call. Then Doug and the team are on top of it again—working toward a conclusion while I'm away.

Systematic Delegation

To make a system like this work, you have to set a precedent and stick to it. If I step back into the process before Doug is ready for me, I could foul up his whole strategy and cancel the decisions that he's already made. Once I've delegated a certain amount of decision making to the team, I have to hold to the policy of letting them *make* those decisions.

As I see it, there are steps to this method that apply to decision making in almost any organization:

1. *Get the right people making decisions.* Each person on your team has certain individual strengths. If you're holding a meeting with people who represent a wide range of expertise, then you want everyone's input. But the person who *actually decides* should be the one person who has the most background and experience in that particular phase of the operation.

Of course you'll want to guide your decision maker to other people inside and outside the organization who can answer questions and influence his decisions. You also have to ask your *own* questions before your team puts a plan into effect, to make sure they haven't overlooked an angle. But the greatest responsibility for the decision is in the hands of the person who knows the most.

2. *Leave the options open.* Sometimes we limit a person's authority and limit his actions just in the way we make assignments. For instance, suppose you tell him: "I want a print media advertising campaign, and I want you to use Agency X." You've already limited his decision-making power in several ways:

· Because you told him it's a "print media campaign," he probably won't consider an advertising campaign in the nonprint media, *even though that may be a better form of advertising for your company.*

· Because you called it an "advertising campaign," he probably won't consider other forms of promotion *even though the other alternatives might be more effective.*

· Because you told him to use Agency X, it's highly unlikely that he will explore the possibility of using Agency Y, *even though Agency Y might do a better job for your company.*

Of course you've made it somewhat easier for your decision maker by limiting the range of choice—but you've also made it less likely that you'll get optimum results from his efforts.

I advocate an open-ended assignment: let decision makers know the goals you want to achieve, then let them figure out the best way to reach those goals. That way, you're *encouraging* decision making from top to bottom, instead of limiting the alternatives. Consider the same assignment expressed in a different way: "I want you to find the best way to give our company visibility and get people to buy our products." That's open-ended. It encourages your people to consider a wide range of possibilities before making a choice. Now they feel free to consider an advertising campaign, a promotion campaign, endorsements, or licensing agreements; they might choose print, TV, direct mail, or some other form of promotion; they might use Agency X, Y, or Z; and, most importantly, they might dream up a way to market your company and your product that you would never have considered.

3. *Skip the "How you doin's!"* In the "how-you-doin' " school

of management, the boss makes the rounds once a day, sticks his head in everyone's office and asks, "How you doin'?" or "How's it goin'?"

It's a nice touch—but it usually doesn't mean much. The boss doesn't really want to know how it's going, because he doesn't have time for any detailed answers to the how-you-doin' question. He has to move along to the *next* office, stick his head in, and ask the same question. Essentially, he's just making a social call. In fact, he may not even be up to date on what his team *is* doing. And he certainly doesn't want anyone on his team to stop him by saying, "I'm stuck . . . I don't know what to do next . . . can you help me out?"

That would ruin his whole day.

The trouble with this management style is that it does more for the boss than it does for the team. It doesn't help anyone solve problems. It doesn't stimulate ideas and it rarely improves performance. It just assures the boss that everything is going fine— whether it is or not—and he feels like a great guy for checking up on everyone. Which, of course, is the way he wants to feel.

If you *really* want to know what's happening, ask something specific about *what each person on your team is doing.* Wait around for the answer. Listen, then deal with it.

If you *don't* want to know—and you don't have time to wait for the answer—DON'T ASK!

4. Suggest additional sources. You can help your decision makers and save them a tremendous amount of time by leading them to people who can help them out with additional information. When I asked John Grant ("Rambo") to set up shore facilities in San Diego for the *Stars & Stripes '88* catamaran, he had to deal with numerous logistics—subleasing the space we wanted to use, clearing out the junk that was there, leveling the area, setting up a machine shop, getting a crane that could lift the catamaran out of the water, and engineering a "flipmobile" that would tilt down the wing and lay it on its side. Rambo knows logistics from the Marines and from the *Stars & Stripes '87* campaign, but '88 posed a whole new set of challenges. We helped him connect with people who knew about everything from leasing to engineering new machinery, and he coordinated the entire effort.

You help your team if you're always on the lookout for sources. When you're looking for the best people and collecting their cards (see page 51), *pass those cards along.* I'll often leave a card on the desk of Rambo, Peter Isler, or Doug Augustine, and suggest, "Give him a call about _____." That way, my decision makers develop their own network of resources.

5. Make sure they don't give away your game. Protecting confidentiality has to be second nature. It goes without saying that there are things you don't want your competitors to know. If your decision maker is unable to recognize that fact, or unable to keep confidential information to himself, no legal document is going to make a difference. Decision makers who can't maintain confidentiality should not be decision makers. In fact, they shouldn't be on your team.

6. Be as tough on them as you want them to be on others. Yes, sometimes there's only one right answer. If you want someone to come back from the negotiating table with $500,000—and that's the minimum—you're not doing your decision maker any favors if you just give him instructions to "do the best you can." How your team negotiates with others will be a fair reflection of what *you* expect of the transaction.

7. Delegate the initiative. You don't just delegate the tasks that have to get done. You also delegate the *initiative* to get things done. When a decision maker comes to you and says, "There are three things wrong with this contract—and here's what they are," you're making progress. But when that person says, "There *were* three things wrong, but I fixed them . . ." you've arrived. He's not only seen the problem, he's taken the initiative.

8. Set a time limit. Anything that protracts a negotiation or delays a decision is a drain on your organization. Your people need to know when you expect the job to be done. If they have a problem, they can come to you, and together you can set a new time limit. Or with the new information in front of you, you may decide to drop the project. But as long as it's alive, the deadlines are always there.

Double Your Power . . . and Double It Again

The leader sets the example. If you withhold information, if you don't trust the people on your team to make decisions, and if you question their judgment—they're likely to treat the people who report to them in exactly the same way. The result, oftentimes, is an organization that is cautious and slow-moving, with employees who are territorial and suspicious.

But if you can delegate the decision-making power along with the resources and support that help people make good decisions, that power gets passed along. They learn from you how to gather information, set goals, consider alternatives, muster the support of other people, and meet a deadline.

So the time you spend teaching people to make good decisions is time well invested. If they, in turn, discover how to delegate decisions, you double your returns—and redouble them again. That kind of return-on-invested time makes for great managers and a powerful organization.

PART 4

Competition

15

Unleash That Competitive Drive!

The Pepsi-Cola Company took a big risk when it decided to become a major sponsor of the 1988 America's Cup campaign. When we met with Mike Lorelli, executive vice president of marketing and national sales at Pepsi, we only had a bare-bones outline of what the America's Cup *might* look like in 1988. We knew the general design of Michael Fay's monohull challenger from New Zealand, but we didn't know exactly how fast it would be. We knew that we wanted to develop a catamaran design to meet the challenge, but when we met with Mike, our design plans were still highly theoretical.

In addition, there were a number of unknown factors—and we had to be straightforward in presenting the unknowns. Would Michael Fay try to introduce other challengers? Would he take us to court over the fairness of our design? Would he agree to the September race date? Or would he do the nearly unthinkable—having challenged us, withdraw from the race?

All these were possibilities. But even so, *we* needed to proceed on the assumption that the race was going to take place, that our boat would be accepted as a valid racing vessel under the Deed of Gift, that Michael Fay would show up, the race would be broadcast on nationwide TV—and, hence, PepsiCo would get nationwide coverage for their sponsorship if they endorsed us.

We presented our case to Mike Lorelli—and he went for it! Why?

Because PepsiCo is in the middle of a battle that's so fierce, so continuous, with so much money at stake, that it makes the America's Cup competition look puny by comparison. *Stars & Stripes* only has to sail the course. But PepsiCo has to fight the eternal cola wars.

Loving the Enemy

"We *love* the cola wars," Mike tells me. "The cola wars are the closest thing to heaven on earth. We make it fun for the consumer while we're on the lookout for a new competitive edge. We don't win every battle. But on average, we gain every year—we narrow the gap. Every once in awhile, we have a big win. I'd say the twenty-four-hour-a-day drive to gain every possible advantage is the *single biggest factor behind our success.*"

Those words, I think, tell the real story behind PepsiCo's backing of the 1988 America's Cup. PepsiCo's desire to win is the same as the *Stars & Stripes'* desire to win. For both of us, it's a gamble—but we can't let the challenge pass. We're in it together because each of us has an enemy out there that we're trying to beat. And we both have that competitive drive.

Who's Got It? Who Doesn't?

Competitive drive takes many different forms. For people like Mike Lorelli at PepsiCo, the drive is not just to gain more market share, but also to be quicker, sharper, more innovative, eye-catching, and dynamic than the other guys. For me, the competitive drive comes from making the commitment, putting in the hard work, and having no excuse to lose—once I've gone that far, I've invested so much into the effort that I've *got* to beat the competition.

For some people, competition means trying to get even with a brother or sister who always won the races or did better in school. Others compete for fame alone; they like the glory that comes with getting the blue ribbon or holding the trophy. You might compete hard because you're trying to achieve a perfect performance or trying to meet some standard of excellence that you've set for yourself. You might compete because you want to get rich. Or you compete because you're fighting for acceptance among your friends, for your parents' approval, or for the respect of someone who always called you the bad guy.

It's important to have some understanding of your own competitive drive for at least two reasons. First, so you can unleash it. Take an extreme example: if the idea of wealth and riches gets your competitive juices flowing, but you go to work at a low salary for a slow-moving company, get ready for a lot of frustration. You'll have to keep your competitive drive under wraps. In order to really unleash that drive, you'd have to join an organization or start a business that lets you combine your competitive drive (to make money) with the goals of the organization (to open new markets or take business away from competitors).

The other reason to understand your own competitive drive is to *see how it's different from others.* It's like motivation. We *don't* all want the same thing—and that's especially important to appreciate when you're putting together a team. One person on your team may be working hard because he's competing with his brother, his cousin, or his father, while the person next to him is working just as hard because he's competing for money, for a big prize, for promotion, or for a perfect performance.

No matter what drives you and your teammates, however, your competitor is your strongest ally. That's right—be *grateful* for a competitor who is innovative, clever, threatening, or dangerous. He's the one who keeps you challenged. If he's good at what he does, he won't let you sleep soundly at night. He alerts you to new possibilities and tests your capabilities. Ultimately, your competitor is the one who keeps *your* head in the game, because he demands more of your skills, talents, and resources than anyone.

As Jack Nicklaus said of Arnold Palmer, your competitor is "always dangerous. You can never lead him by too many shots."

There are three steps to making yourself an effective competitor: (1) Find your own strengths; (2) Watch your competitor's mistakes; (3) Take the inside track.

1. FIND YOUR OWN STRENGTHS

Each of us has our personal strengths and weaknesses that show up in how we perform, how we work with a team, how we organize people, and how we compete. The better you know your strengths and capitalize on them, the better you'll do competitively. This is true whether you're an entrepreneur starting up your own company; a big company offering a new product; an employee competing for promotion; or an athlete in competition.

The Entrepreneur

If you're starting a small business and competing against established companies or the giants in the market, it's essential to find your own niche. What is it that your company does particularly well? What product or service can you offer to consumers that they're not getting elsewhere? What's the *particular strength* that gives you the competitive edge?

When CB Vaughan started his line of ski pants, the large established skiwear manufacturers were all going after the same big accounts—the Bloomingdale's, Macy's, and Nieman-Marcuses. CB knew he didn't stand a chance trying to launch his line in the big department stores. That wasn't his strength. He didn't have a track record, inventory, or a long product line. So he packed his ski pants into the trunk of his car and started selling to all the *little* shops in Vermont.

When Paul Hawken and David Smith started the Smith & Hawken garden tool business in California, they faced competition from all the garden tool manufacturers in the United States. A few large manufacturers supplied most of the garden centers, hardware supply stores, and retail chains. To knock even one of those well-known suppliers out of position would have cost Smith & Hawken a fortune that they didn't have.

But big merchandising wasn't their strength. From the very beginning, Paul Hawken decided that the only way to penetrate the market was to supply consumers with better *quality* gardening tools than they could find anywhere else—even if customers had to pay more for those tools. Smith & Hawken opened their company in an industrial warehouse in Palo Alto, with 2,500 sturdy English garden tools, and then they launched their merchandising effort by placing selected ads in gardening publications. Their first catalog of tools, which cost $12,700 to produce, was mailed to gardeners who responded to the magazine ads.

Smith & Hawken stuck to what they saw as their strength; they sold people on the quality of their tools and service. Because they built on their strengths, they were able to compete successfully. Within five years, Smith & Hawken was doing $2.4 million in sales.

The Big Competitor

For a big competitor in a crowded market, the key is *careful positioning* to sell your product or service. Where are your greatest strengths? What are the most outstanding features of whatever you're offering the customer? Why should someone choose you over a competitor? It's important to answer those questions for yourself before you launch your offensive.

In recent years, all the Big Eight accounting firms have become involved in worldwide financial consulting, a new addition to their traditional auditing activities. In a market that commands billions of dollars annually, the competition for new business is fierce. Of all the arenas of financial services, the competition on Wall Street is fiercest.

In 1982 the accounting firm of Touche Ross opened a new Financial Services Center targeted precisely to get Wall Street business. The opening of the new office was carefully strategized.

Tom Presby, the former executive director of Touche Ross International, was selected to create a financial center that would be "a model of the eighties consultative practice." Management gave him carte blanche to use all the Touche Ross resources to launch this full-scale attack on the New York financial services market.

Presby took three steps. First, he flew around the country recruiting the best managers and partners from inside TR—those most experienced in brokerage and banking. Presby offered attractive promotions, bonuses, and salary increases if the top performers would move to New York—and they went for it! Secondly, he broke with Touche Ross tradition by making the new Financial Services Center a completely separate and independent practice. Thirdly, Presby made sure that the Financial Services Center would offer a wide range of services. Within the Center, he opened up Financial Advisory Services, Regulatory Consulting, an Audit Group, a Management Consulting Group, Financial Advisory Services, and Reorganization Advisory Services.

Opening the new office was a ten-million-dollar proposition, but it quickly became a major presence on Wall Street. Positioned as "a full-service accounting firm that happens to do audits," the Financial Services Center was aggressively marketed. By playing up its main feature—"full-service accounting"—Touche Ross created a position for itself in one of the toughest markets in the world.

Unlike CB Vaughan or Smith & Hawken, Touche Ross had millions of dollars to spend in a frontal attack on a crowded market. Because the scale was different, so was the tactic. Instead of finding a niche, Touche Ross had to establish a strong, broad-based position from the very beginning. The firm put the best resources behind the effort—and the bold move paid off.

The Employee

If you're competing for position, salary, or promotion inside your own company, the key to getting the competitive advantage is to *find a strength and build on it!*

In the midseventies, the branch manager of a Boston bank saw that Automatic Teller Machines (ATMs) were the wave of the future. The bank he worked for was locked in traditionalism, and he knew it would be some time before ATMs won acceptance. But he foresaw that change was inevitable—and he also foresaw that the person with the most knowledge about ATMs would be in a preferred list for advancement.

During the next two years, the branch manager found out everything he could about ATM operations. He became a specialist. He was promoted to the central office. And when the bank finally made the decision to install ATMs in all its branch offices, the young manager was promoted (over thirty-five other managers) to the position of vice president of operations.

If you're competing for position, look at the other people who might be promoted ahead of you. Ask yourself: What is my particular strength? What can I do better than any of them? When you find that strength, build on it—get the education, training, or experience you need to go farther.

The Athlete

Most athletes are strong in one area of competition, less so in others. For the professional or the amateur athlete, it's essential to stick to the area where you're strongest.

In 1968, going into the Olympics, Mark Spitz was considered the best swimmer in the United States. George Haynes, the coach of the 1968 U.S. Olympic swimming team, predicted that Spitz would win as many as six gold medals. In Mexico City, however, Spitz only won two gold medals—both in relay events—along with a silver in the 100-meter butterfly and a bronze medal for third place in the 100-meter freestyle. It was widely considered a disappointing performance, and Mark Spitz was more disappointed than anyone. That experience made him look closely at the way he was managing his athletic career. It forced him to analyze his personal strengths and weaknesses.

Four years later, at the Munich Olympics, he returned to

become the most successful athlete in Olympic history by winning seven gold medals in swimming.

In those four years, Mark had surrounded himself with people who could coach him, manage his career, and handle the publicity and public relations. That way, Mark Spitz could concentrate on his single greatest strength—competitive swimming.

He had learned a valuable lesson about competitive performance. In any kind of athletics, what happens during the game is only part of the competition. There are many other things that go along with it—publicity, promotion, financing, travel, and management, to name just a few. But athletes cannot be all things to all people. They need to concentrate on what they do best— and delegate the rest.

2. WATCH YOUR COMPETITOR'S MISTAKES

At the same time that you're discovering your own strengths, you have to learn about your competitor's weaknesses—by observing, by competing, or by hearing about those weaknesses from others.

Donald Trump, the premier deal maker among New York's multimillionaires, has put together numerous real estate deals, culminating in the Trump Tower in Manhattan and Trump Casino in Atlantic City. He is constantly watching for the weaknesses of his competitors.

"I watch other people," he told me. "I study them and learn from their mistakes. If you see what those mistakes are, you don't have to make them yourself. If somebody makes a faulty move, you try not to make that move in your own vocabulary."

On the sailing course, we're always watching for our competitor's mistake. It may happen only once during a race—when he decides to tack right and misses getting a lift, or when he drops his spinnaker a little too soon before the mark—but that one mistake might cost him the race. We *watch* him, and when we see that mistake, we make sure we don't make the same move.

3. TAKE THE INSIDE TRACK

In business, favorable timing, luck, or a change in plans might give you the inside track. When you *see* that inside track—go for it! For instance:

• Suppose you're looking for a promotion in your company, but you don't have as much seniority as someone else who's competing for the same position. Then you hear about a project that's going to lead to a new line of business. It just so happens that you're meeting with the president at nine o'clock; you find out your main rival for the promotion won't be meeting with him until afterward.

There's the inside track! That nine-o'clock meeting gives you the opportunity to tell the president about your interest in the new project. Ask to be considered for the position of project director. Talk about it. Tell the boss how much you'd like to head up the team that takes on the project, how hard you'd work, and what a great job you'd do. You *want* it—so unleash that competitive drive!

• Suppose you're a salesperson who's been calling on a prospect for a year and getting nowhere. Your competitor seems to be firmly entrenched in the company you're calling on. You need a break if you're going to have your offer taken seriously.

Then you find out that your competitor's company has gone on strike—for the first time in twenty years. As the strike drags on, your competitor's deliveries are delayed. You know the customer needs your kind of product, and if he's not going to get it from your competitor, the customer has to get it from you!

There's the inside track. Double your sales efforts. Use all your contacts. Improve your price. Sell the prospect on the benefits of working with your company. Keep on the inside track until you get that account.

• Suppose you want to be nominated for a position on a committee, but your name hasn't been mentioned yet. Then you learn that your mentor (who is one of your biggest allies) is planning to have lunch with the chairman of the committee.

Should you talk to your mentor? Tell him how much you want to be on that committee? Of course! Let your mentor know how important a committee seat is to you, how much you want to serve.

Opportunities Aren't Forever

You may have only one opportunity—that nine-o'clock meeting with the boss, a strike at your competitor's company, a meeting between your mentor and the committee chairman. *Don't assume that a second opportunity will ever arise!* Consider that opportunity as your *only chance* to get the inside track. And when you've got it—unleash that competitive drive!

16

Don't Believe the
Odds Against You

On Tuesday, October 20, 1987, *USA Today* looked at the odds for and against the St. Louis Cardinals winning the World Series. On that day, as they headed back for their home field, the Cards were down 2–0 in their series against the Minnesota Twins. Sports writers and commentators were going wild with the statistics. They were trying to calculate the chances of the Cardinals coming back to win in six or seven games. What were the chances of the Cards' left-hander, John Tudor, winning game #3 to keep the Cards in the running? What was the home team advantage? How had the Twins performed in the past when they were on the road?

Here's how the statisticians at *USA Today* measured the odds:

OVERALL . . .

- Only 9 out of 35 teams that lost the first two games of the World Series ended up winning. So the odds against the Cardinals were about 4 to 1.

IN FAVOR OF THE CARDS . . .

- The Twins' record was 31–53 on the road.
- Playing on real turf on the road, the Twins' record was only 5–14 (.263).
- The Twins starter, Les Straker, only won 2 out of 7 on the road with a 4.57 ERA.
- The Twins blew a 2–0 lead in the 1965 World Series.

IN FAVOR OF THE TWINS . . .

- Three of the Twins' team members regularly hit better on the road than at home—Greg Gagne (.289 road, .241 home), Steve Lombardozzi (.265 road, .211 home), and Kirby Puckett (.362 road, .301 home).
- The Twins had a good record against left-handers: 26–17 (.605).

Now, if you consider all these statistics, factor in wind speed and humidity and the injury of St. Louis's designated hitter; further factor in the umpire who had a fight with his wife that morning and is ready to botch a call; measure the volume of home team catcalls coming from the stadium; and divide by an unknown percentage of error, you might be able to predict the outcome of games 3, 4, 5, 6, and 7, and the teams could go home without even bothering to play the remaining games.

But what do the odds *actually* mean to the players on the field?

What do they mean to pitcher John Tudor the next day when he steps up to the mound?

And what do the Game 3 odds mean in the fifth inning of Game 7, when St. Louis and Minnesota are 3–3 in games and 2–2 in the final game?

By the end of that World Series, as we now know, the chances of St. Louis winning were, in fact, 0 out of 100. That's right. *The Cards did not win.* The record book shows that, by the final out, their chances of winning had boiled down to 0 in 100.

Odds Are Ancient History

Statistics are great for pundits, and writers, and commentators. They might make betting easier. But to the people who play the game, *statistics are ancient history.* They only record past actions; they don't predict future performance.

If you're up at bat, you only have two options: you can hit the ball . . . or not. If you're a fielder, you can catch it or not catch it. If you're a pitcher, you have your choice of how to throw the ball on every pitch. How you hit, how you field, and how you pitch is not some *average* derived from past performance. It's based on what you can do *right now.*

Actual performance is not *based on* the odds.

Performance *changes* the odds.

That's why *you should never believe the odds are against you.*

Don't Believe the Odds in Your Favor, Either

Maybe I'm fortunate to be in a sport that is *not* inundated with statistics. But at one time in my career, there was one, overwhelming statistic that everyone but me seemed to believe. Going into the 1983 America's Cup, the statistic was this:

> The United States has never lost an America's Cup. *Therefore, we have a 100 percent chance of winning it again in 1983.*

The New York Yacht Club believed that statistic.

Most of the yachting press believed it.

People all across America, some of whom had only the vaguest idea what the America's Cup was about, believed it.

Sometimes it seemed that the only person who realized the real chances of winning against *Australia II* was Dennis Conner. (Plus the people on my team who knew all too well, from actual observation, that Australia had a faster boat.)

Now how can the odds be 100–0 in your favor if you're racing against an opponent with a faster boat? Those odds were *history.*

I couldn't believe the odds that everyone else believed. I had to *believe the odds as I saw them.*

The way I saw it, unless the Australians were thrown out of the race on the basis of breaking design rules, *the odds were against us winning.*

And I was right.

See Your Percentage Points in the Present

Tom Whidden, who has probably sailed alongside me more often than any other person on earth, once told a writer, "Dennis is very good at measuring the percentage points."

Here's what Tom was saying: *We make up our own odds as we see them.*

I don't mean "make them up" out of thin air. I mean, we get as much information as we can, talk to people who know what's happening, train, test, work out, perform, and then we try to be as realistic as possible about the percentages.

If we can go out in the morning and improve our boat speed with a new sail, our odds might increase .01 percent. If that new sail improves boat speed for ten straight days in conditions that vary all over the place, then our odds have increased a couple of percentage points and I'm happy. I'll start looking for other areas where we can add a point or two in our favor.

Now, the competition doesn't know I've improved my odds, because they don't know what I'm up to. The press doesn't know, because I don't tell them either. The sportswriters and forecasters don't know, because their forecasts are based on past history and best-guesses. But Dennis and Tom Whidden and the guys on the boat know we just improved our game, and that means we improved our odds of winning, even though our competitor knows nothing about it.

Sun Tzu, the Chinese philosopher who wrote *The Art of War*, summed it up: "When we are near, we make it appear that we are far away; when far away, that we are near."

The Past Does Not Predict the Future!

No matter what you do—in sports, business, family life, education, arts, entertainment—*don't believe the odds against you!*

If you believe the odds that you hear, you're using history to predict the future. You're planting a message in your own mind that says, "Yeah, they're right, my chances are only one in a hundred (or one in a thousand, or one in a million)."

That might be true when you're starting out. But you can improve your odds every day. There's no magic to this. You can be smart about it. Odds will never be a hundred percent in your favor, but there are lots of ways you can work them in that direction.

For instance, if you are thinking about starting up a small business, you must be aware that of the half-million small businesses that start up every year, about sixty percent will fail in the second to fifth year. So what are your chances of making it from the second to fifth year if you start up a small business?

You might think your chances are 4 in 10. But that's not accurate.

You haven't told me what your business is yet. You haven't told me what your product is, how you're going to market it, how much start-up cash you have, and how you're going to build the business if it's successful. In order to accurately predict your chances, someone would have to know who you're going to hire, how much advertising you're going to do, and whether you're really *committed* to the new business.

All these are factors in the success of the business. So are your ability to sell, your ability to convince your suppliers that you're going to grow and become profitable, and your ability to convince people to take a risk with you.

None of this is scientific, of course, and there is no single factor that *guarantees* your success in a start-up business. But everything you have going in your favor improves your odds. Your product decisions, your pricing, your sales strategy, your determination, and your flexibility all affect your chances of making it.

Whether you're a large company or small, the odds improve as people on your team *set about improving them.* Twenty years ago, who would have said that a Japanese motorcycle company had any chance of selling cars in the United States? But Soichiro Honda believed it was possible—and everyone at Honda set about improving the percentages, until the odds of success were finally a hundred percent in his favor.

Who would have believed that anyone could sell Pet Rocks to the American public? The odds were about 1,000 to 1. But in 1975 an unemployed commercial artist and copywriter living in Los Gatos, California, began to talk about Pet Rocks to some of his buddies at the Grog & Sirloin bar. A few weeks later, he was designing a carrying case, complete with a handle and breathing holes, with a Pet Rock inside. He set about improving the odds until his once-penniless company (called Rock Bottom) was selling 100,000 rocks a day.

How to Turn the Odds in Your Favor

If you're competitive, you will always be looking for ways to raise the odds in your own favor.

But how do you do that? What can you do to improve your percentages every day?

There are at least three steps: (1) Do more repetitions; (2) Be savvy about your chances; and (3) Get off to a better start.

1. DO MORE REPETITIONS

Who has more chance of being a big-league pitcher—the guy who does ten pitches a day, or the guy who does a hundred? One hundred pitches a day is no *guarantee* that you're going to make the Padres, but it certainly ups the odds in your favor. Given a competitor with equal talent, *you have the advantage* if you do the repetitions.

In business, as in sports, repetitions improve your odds. Some of the ways in which you might become more competitive are:

- Research more subjects.
- Write more reports.
- Talk to more experts.
- Read more books.
- Practice your skills more often.
- Visit your customers more often.

Quantity isn't everything. But you definitely increase the odds in your favor if you *repeatedly* perform in ways that pay off for you and your organization.

2. BE SAVVY ABOUT YOUR CHANCES

Technically, seventy percent of one hundred percent is exactly the same as one hundred percent of seventy percent. In other words, if you expect to win ten blue ribbons and you only win seven—or if you hope to win seven ribbons and you *do* win seven—either way, you've won seven ribbons.

Technically, yes. But *mentally* it's not the same. If you wanted to win all ten, you walk away disappointed if you only win seven. On the other hand, if you only hoped for seven and you *got* seven, you're elated. You won everything you wanted!

Habitually, we compare what we *want* to what we've *got*—so we never really see things in terms of absolute numbers. We only see them in terms of how well we *see ourselves doing*—matched in terms of our expectations or matched against the competition.

Robert Strauss, former chairman of the National Democratic Committee (1973–76), is a consummate negotiator and power broker in Washington circles. The founder of the prestigious Texas law firm of Akin, Gump, Strauss, Hauer and Feld, Robert Strauss maintains a Washington office, where he is known as a troubleshooter who can always "make things happen."

With his potent influence in Washington circles, Bob Strauss is constantly consulting politicians, corporate chiefs, and policy makers who are out to *measure the odds.* When a client comes to him with a goal that stands very little chance of being achieved, Strauss may say, "Mr. Smith, you might not get one hundred percent of what you want. But I think I can get you sixty percent. We'll stay within the realm of what we can achieve."

People come to Strauss because he has a reputation for making the deal work. He's playing the odds, but in a way that gets *positive* results rather than producing *negative* results. He won't promise one hundred percent of anything if he doesn't think it's possible; instead, he'll give that client a more realistic chance of getting sixty percent. Then, if the client ends up getting *seventy percent*, he's *won* rather than *lost*.

Be realistic about your odds. If you judge the percentages right, you set yourself up to succeed. When we were planning the '88 campaign, we looked at our odds carefully before we settled on a boat design. We figured we had a very low chance of successfully designing and testing an eighty or ninety-foot catamaran in the time we had. However, when we looked over all the options, we figured we had a very *good* chance of successfully designing a sixty-foot catamaran. In other words, just by deciding to go with a sixty-foot boat, we increased the odds of success to nearly one hundred percent.

3. GET OFF TO A BETTER START

Another way to improve your odds of competitive success is by getting off to a great start. Even though the fleet tries to out-tack and outmaneuver you during the race, the competitor with the better start has an early advantage. Whether you're competing for yourself or whether you're leading a team, a crew, or a company, you can stack the odds in your favor by crossing the starting line on the right tack: approach a challenge with the best solution for the job, and position yourself ahead of the competition.

Donald Trump demonstrated this beautifully in 1986 when he made a deal with the City of New York to renovate Wollman Rink, the ice-skating rink in Central Park. For six years, contractors hired by the city had been attempting to renovate the rink.

From its inception, the city project had been plagued by incompetent management, faulty design, poor engineering, entirely avoidable delays, breakdowns, and cost overruns.

When Donald Trump offered to take over the project, he *set the condition* that he would complete it within six months and bring it in under cost . . . or pay the difference. The first thing Donald did was call the top guy at Cimco, the Toronto-based company that built the rink for the Montreal Canadiens. Cimco was the logical choice to build refrigeration and piping and provide consultation on the project.

From the experts at Cimco, Donald found out that the city's plan for the rink *had never stood much chance of success.* The city had decided to use a Freon system, while most of the rinks in the country used a more reliable and very durable brine system. The Freon system used new technology and was difficult to maintain. The brine system cost somewhat more to run, but it was far more reliable.

By the time Donald got off the phone, he had decided to install the brine system. *That single decision* got the whole project started where it should have been in the first place.

Donald then hired HRH, the company that had built Trump Tower and the Hyatt, to do the construction work. And Ice Capades took over management of the rink when it opened.

The result: the rink was completed nearly a month ahead of the six-month schedule, and public use of the rink increased by a factor of ten.

Anyone going by the *history* of the project would have said it was a six-year project . . . at least. Donald Trump completed it in less than *six months.* He changed *all* the odds, just by getting off to the right start.

The Future Potential

If you do more repetitions, you're savvy about your chances, and you get off to a better start, you really do improve your odds of winning.

Of course, there's always the danger of overconfidence or underconfidence. If you look at past performance and your record of wins is high, you may easily (and understandably) become overconfident about how well you'll do tomorrow. On the other hand, if your past record shows a lot of losses, you could get discouraged by the way the odds seemed to be stacked against you.

The best policy is to *blind yourself to the odds of the past.* Concentrate on present odds, and find ways to improve them in the future. The odds of yesterday are just math—but to measure what the odds may be tomorrow, you have to measure your own potential. And your potential increases astronomically if *you don't believe the odds against you!*

17

Keep an Eye on the Competition

If I were in the New York real estate business, I would be following Donald Trump's every move. I would want to know everything he was doing before other people knew, and I'd always be asking, "*Why* is he making that move?"

Because Donald Trump is doing something right.

And if you're competing with someone like that, I believe you always have to *keep an eye on the competition.*

Watch—Don't Imitate

I don't mean that you can imitate someone's style or copy his moves. The trouble with taking a photocopy of someone else's game plan is that you don't understand it from the inside out; it's not the result of your own experiences, observations, and conclusions.

But if you pick out what your competitor is doing *right* and try it out in your own language, you can learn from your competitor's successes as well as from his mistakes. You can find out what he's thinking about and why he's making certain moves. You can even

155

anticipate some of his moves—the old art of beating-him-to-the-punch.

When Paul Hawken and David Smith had been in business for about a year, some of the big tool companies began to produce knockoffs that closely resembled (in appearance, but not quality) some of the fine English gardening tools that Smith & Hawken was marketing. Seeing where their competitors were trying to move in, the entrepreneurs responded instantly by cutting prices and increasing their promotional efforts. They won that round *by keeping their eye on the competition.*

When Pepsi-Cola learned that Coca-Cola was about to release a storm of publicity surrounding the introduction of "New Coke," the marketing people at Pepsi explored every avenue to find out details about the new product. Had the Coke people *really* changed the formula? Why were they willing to take this huge gamble? What would happen to Pepsi's advertising claim (proven in taste tests), that Pepsi's flavor was the one preferred by consumers? Everyone on the Pepsi team knew their assignment: *keep an eye on the competition.*

In a sailing race against a fleet of boats, we look in two directions—up front, to the guy we're trying to catch, and behind, to the guys who are trying to catch *us.* Someone, at all times, *has his eye on the competition.*

If you're *Time,* you keep an eye on *Newsweek.*

If you're Macy's, you watch Bloomingdale's.

If you're Federal Express, you keep an eye on Emery.

If your hotdog stand is on the east side of the street, you watch what happens on the west side.

Whenever I hear a salesperson say, "I don't worry about the competition," I know he's stupid, he's lying, or he's been fed too much of his own company's propaganda.

AT&T didn't worry about MCI.

GM didn't worry about Ford.

IBM didn't worry about Apple or DEC.

But they're worried now.

It doesn't matter how big you are: if there's one all-American lesson, it's that the competition can always sneak up on you. They can do it by being smarter, quicker, or more innovative. They can do it by working harder. Or they can try something you never thought of trying yourself.

Study What Your Competitor is Doing Right

If you have a highly successful competitor, you have an opportunity for a short, free education course. When Vince Lombardi gave an eight-hour lecture on the Green Bay Sweep, John Madden listened and watched attentively. It was a big opportunity to get an education in what his competitor was doing right.

When I finally got photographs of *Australia II*'s keel, I studied those photos like the rulebook: that was the keel that beat us, and I wanted to know everything about it. Essentially, my competitor gave me a complete education in how to design a keel that would allow a boat to go faster. It would have been ungrateful of me *not* to get an education from that.

If I wanted to build a better mousetrap, the first thing I would do is get hold of the best mousetrap on the market. I would look at the packaging to find out why people are buying this mousetrap. I'd test it out. I'd take it apart. *Then* I'd go to the drawing board and find out whether I could design an improved mousetrap.

It's all part of studying your competitor's game and understanding what he's trying to do. Once you know, you may decide to use what you learn; you may decide that your own way is better; or you may decide that you can surpass him by using some of his innovations along with the skills you already have. But whatever you do, *you can't ignore what he's up to.*

You Can Always Be Challenged

In a competitive sport or a competitive market, it's easy to get complacent if you're in the lead. But you can always be blindsided, no matter how small or insignificant a challenger may look at first. Many large, well-established companies have learned, to their chagrin, the high cost of becoming too complacent.

A few years ago, Apollo Computer of Chelmsford, Massachusetts, had what it considered an unassailable position in the market. It was the sole producer of computer workstations—that is, individual desktop computers that are hooked up with each other and with a central network. In 1982 Apollo had no real competitors in a growing market niche.

In 1982, two friends from Stanford Business School, twenty-seven-year-old Scott McNealy and India-born Vinod Khosla, founded Sun Microsystems, in Mountain View, California. To Apollo, Sun didn't look like a competitor at all—McNealy and Khosla didn't even have the resources to produce their own computers.

But McNealy and Khosla didn't *intend* to build their own. Instead, they used off-the-shelf components and put together cheap, flexible designs that fit with whatever computer equipment was already installed. There were two advantages to this approach: they could build computers that were compatible with their competitor's products, and they could install the most up-to-date technology in the field. "The approach," observed *Fortune* magazine, "has enabled the company to double the computing speed of its workstations every year."

From 1983 to 1987, Sun grew from $9 million to $538 million in sales, with an average growth rate of 127 percent a year. It rolled right over Apollo and every other competitor. In 1987 Sun was the second fastest-growing company in America. Khosla retired at age 30, and McNealy is now president, with 6,500 employees in his company.

The Sun Microsystems story is not just another example of exponential growth in the high-tech field. Instead, it's the story of a complacent giant (Apollo) that failed to keep an eye on the competition (Sun).

But Apollo is paying attention now.

Change—Or Hold Your Course?

Keeping an eye on a competitor doesn't mean you change your tactics every time he changes his. In fact, trying to imitate your competitor or change your style can have disastrous results. IBM has its own distinctive corporate culture. It can meet Apple, Compaq, Wang, Burroughs, NCR, DEC, or any of its other competitors in the marketplace and go head-to-head with them for sales. But if IBM tried to refashion its corporate structure to match DEC's style, the employees of Big Blue would go into culture shock.

Business changes occur so rapidly that it's impossible to stand still. You have to be alert to the competition, but at the same time, you have to move in your own way. So while you have to be poised to change your course, you must also be prepared to analyze whether your course is the right one—and whether you should stick to it.

In a study of "peak performers" in business, technology, and sports, psychologist Charles Garfield—one of the men who worked on the Apollo II mission—noted that every peak performer has the ability to make *course corrections.* Garfield observed that "effective course correction depends on accurate information about (a) yourself, (b) the organization, (c) macroforces—the industry, the economy, the world situation."

The key word here, as I see it, is "information." If you know what you can do, you know the capabilities of your organization, and you've studied your competitor, then you're probably equipped with enough hard information to make a good course correction. But if any information is lacking, you really have to get the data before you make a decision.

Once you have that information, how do you decide whether or not to change course? In a competitive market, here are some factors to consider:

1. Is that new entry in the market ultimately going to get your competitor in trouble?

Your competitor may launch a deceptively large PR or advertising campaign to launch a new product. Sometimes it's difficult *not* to believe the hype—but important to make your own judgment. When the executives at Pepsi had their first taste of New Coke, they were relieved. Despite all the buildup for the new product, *in their judgment* they felt that the new taste wasn't as good as traditional Coke. So Pepsi based its counterattack on the assumption that consumers wouldn't accept the New Coke as a replacement.

Use your own criteria to judge whether you think a product is going to prove successful. Try to see it from the consumer's point of view—apart from all the promotion. Can your competitor actually *deliver* what he says he can?

2. Will there be anything left for the guy who comes in second?

In some areas of competition, coming in second is just as good as coming in first. Avis is still not as big as Hertz, but there's plenty of room in the market for both companies to be very profitable.

On the other hand, playing follow-the-leader can get you in trouble if the market is saturated or consumers simply aren't interested in a competitive alternative. If your competitor has the advantage of advance secrecy and perfect timing, it may be impossible to catch up with him. Better to pursue what you do best and remain consistent, rather than chase after a market that may already be saturated.

3. Does your competitor have a second- and third-wave assault planned?

A competitor who has worked with all due speed and secrecy to introduce a new product is likely to have plans for follow-up—using data that he gathers from the first-wave assault. If you see a product that would be the *logical next development* of your competitor's, be suspicious! Ask yourself: has he already thought of it? Does he already have plans to take the next step?

If you are planning to anticipate his next move, you might consider leapfrogging—hopping *over* the next step to a line of products or a consumer approach that he hasn't even thought of yet.

H. Ross Perot, one of the most successful entrepreneurs in recent business history, was originally a salesman for IBM. At a time when IBM was primarily supplying computers and software, he saw an opportunity to get into the business of offering complete data processing services to companies. Perot suggested the idea at IBM, but his suggestion was turned down—and that's when he struck out on his own, building a multibillion-dollar company that sold services rather than products.

Essentially, Perot was two jumps ahead of the game. There was an established market for computers; a growing market for software; but the market for computer services was completely untapped, and Perot got there first.

4. Is your competitor feeding a fad—or finding a trend?

In any market, *fads* are different from *trends.* It's important to recognize the difference. Fads can come and go so quickly that by the time you leap into the market and try to catch up, the fad may be over. The hula-hoop was a great fad, but some entrepreneurs mistook it for a trend. When people stopped buying hula-hoops, a number of competitors started producing hula-hoop lookalikes—and ended up bankrupt.

But the hula-hoop fad indicated a *trend* toward novelty toys. Many companies that got into that market by offering a wide range of novelty toys have been successful. They understood the trend and took advantage of it.

Prepare Your Defense Your Own Way

When you're in the lead, a competitive challenge can come suddenly, from any quarter. Your competitor's style may be brash and reckless. It could be dangerous and hard-hitting. Or smooth, overbearing, well oiled, and well financed.

When the challenge comes, your mentors, your coaches, your assistants, your advisors, your consultants, or your employees can help you prepare your defense—up to a point. After that, it's up to you. *You* have to decide how to meet that challenge. You may have to move fast, use your instincts, and take a gamble based on experience. But whatever you do, meet that challenge *your own way*—not in a way that imitates your challenger's style.

"Trust your stomach," is the way PepsiCo's Mike Lorelli puts it. "Surround yourself with people who complement your skills. Listen to all advice and hear all opinions. Your mind has to collect all the data, then send the results to your stomach. *You have to trust your own judgment.*

"And no matter what happens, keep getting up to bat."

Throughout his career, Arnold Palmer was greatly influenced by Ben Hogan—a player whom he respected as one of the best technical golfers who ever swung a club. But Palmer discovered that he had to trust his *own* game.

"Every time I have ever been in a tight spot, I have tried to play the way I know best, to be aggressive, to go back to my natural game. I am not a Hogan. And I can't play Hogan's way. I've had to tell myself, 'Hey, stop trying to play Hogan, and play Palmer. Your way is the best for you.' "

Sometimes, especially in a moment of panic, you may be tempted to mirror your competitor. But when you mirror his or her moves, you lose the initiative that comes with playing the game your own way. You might successfully mirror the first move . . . and the second . . . but as long as you're *re*acting instead of *acting,* you're on the defensive. That means you'll always be a step or two behind.

After all, your competitor has been out there practicing those moves—you haven't. Find your own style and use it!

18

Be Glad They're
Tough to Beat

Over the years, I've been fortunate to meet most of the toughest competitors in the world of sailing. To mention only a few:

· Malin Burnham, a San Diego sailor and the president of Sail America, is a great sportsman and a great businessman. He won the Star Boat Worlds at age seventeen with Lowell North (age fifteen) as his crew. For years, he and North were the ones to beat. They were more than just tough competitors—they were an inspiration to everyone who sailed.

· Ted Turner. I've been part of his crew, and I've sailed against him in offshore races and America's Cup competition. A talented sailor with personal drive and ambition, the founder of CNN has the kind of energy and enthusiasm that gets people to reach new heights of performance. Above all, he gets personally involved and *makes things happen.*

· Alan Bond. I have great admiration for this multimillionaire Australian businessman who took away the Cup from us in 1983 and mounted a great defense in '87. A high school dropout who turned a real estate business into a successful, multimillion-dollar diversified corporation, Bond is an unstoppable optimist. He con-

163

ceived the idea of mounting a bid for the America's Cup in 1970: four boats, thirteen years, and sixteen million dollars later, he got what he wanted.

• Chris Dickson. At age twenty-three, the skipper of the New Zealand boat in America's Cup '87 showed leadership, persistence, courage, and equanimity during the round-robins and the finals. Although New Zealand was a new contender in '87, under Dickson's command the Kiwis gave *Stars & Stripes* our toughest competition—and Dickson showed style and humor when both were needed.

• Michael Fay. New Zealand's powerful merchant banker used every conceivable legal maneuver, psychological tactic, and media strategy to seize the Cup from the San Diego Yacht Club in 1988. As part of his tactics, New Zealand has launched one of the most innovative monohull designs in recent sailing history— and he has tested our resources, our patience, and our ingenuity to the limits.

These are only a few of those who have challenged me and my crews; made my days long and my nights short; forced me to come up with better ideas and to work harder at my strategies; ruined some days (when I lost); *made* other days (when I won); given me chances at fame; made me mad; made me happy; tested everything I've got; and (usually) shaken hands with me after each competition was over.

Though radically different from each other in style, performance, and character, there is one thing they all have in common: they were tough to beat.

Your toughest competitors are your biggest allies in the art of winning. They're the ones who make you work harder, move faster, and think smarter. They test your nerves, test your patience, and try your ingenuity. They raise the stakes and, by challenging you to the limits of your ability, raise the level of competition. In the heat of the game, of course, we don't feel any particular gratitude toward those competitors. But when it's all over—if the game has been fairly played—we have more than enough reasons to be grateful that they tested us.

Tough competitors have different competitive styles—that's one of the things that keeps the competition interesting. Each can pose a new threat—or mount a different kind of challenge. To prepare to meet those challenges, we have to understand our competitors and prepare appropriately for the competition. In my years of sailing and business dealings, here are some competitive "types" that I've been able to identify:

THE MENTOR

Typically, he's an older person at the peak of his form who gives you advice. If you're lucky, you meet him when you're still the young go-getter, trying to learn all you can, get ahead, and compete with people at your level of play. At first, this person is so many levels above you that you might not even consider him a competitor. He appears to be a complete master of the game.

Getting attached to an experienced advisor early in your career, or in the early levels of competition, can be the greatest boon of your life. For a time, the mentor can literally teach you "all you have to know." But there comes a time, too, when the mentor becomes a competitor—when you start to approach that level of the game you thought you could never reach, and you become a serious challenger.

THE CHALLENGE: To develop your own competitive style. If you have worked with the mentor for a number of years—or if he's someone you have watched and tried to learn from—there's a temptation to remain a perpetual "student." In fact, it may be a revelation to discover that there are moves he doesn't know and things he can't do—but you can! When you make that discovery—when you begin to flex your own muscles and use all your resources—you break away from becoming a learner and start to come into your own.

THE ENERGIZER

The Energizer is a tough competitor because he combines enthusiasm, charisma, forcefulness, and determination in a winning personality. That combination makes him an effective leader, someone who has a high tolerance for disappointment and a tremendous will to achieve. Typically, this competitor throws his energy into *any* kind of enterprise with verve and determination. He rallies people to his cause; maintains a high profile; creates great press for himself and his team; and meets every crisis with an air of impeccable, can't-lose optimism.

One temptation, particularly risky for anyone who competes against the energizer, is attempting to imitate his style. The energizer's magnetism is so strong, and he is so adept at winning people to his side, that he appears to get all the lucky breaks. It's easy to fall into the trap of becoming envious of trying to emulate his style rather than developing strategies that are uniquely your own.

THE CHALLENGE: Competing with the energizer requires, above all, patience. You may not be able to match him at the peak of his high energy, but in the long run you may get a higher payoff from showing more stamina, exercising more concentration, or being more thorough in your preparations. It's easy to be misled by the way the energizer attracts people and rallies them to his cause: the same high-energy behavior that lures them in the first place may turn them off when it gets to burnout time, or when the energizer's attention swings wildly in another direction. If you have a team that trusts your leadership and is loyal to you over the long haul, you ultimately have the competitive advantage.

On the other hand, the energizer should alert you to *your* own energy level. To meet his challenge, you may have to become more energetic and enthusiastic in your performance. You have to get people charged up. You have to create enthusiasm. Get the news out: create some great PR for yourself. Get the press on your side. Rally the good guys to support you. If you've got energy *and* endurance, the one-note energizer doesn't stand a chance against you.

THE MOGUL

The mogul has comfortable access to money, power, and influence. He can summon the right people to his side with one or two phone calls. If you decide to compete with him, he may attempt to knock you out of position primarily by wielding influence.

This competitor is frustrating, especially in business, because his position seems so protected and unassailable. If he's better connected and better funded than you are, he may seem too powerful to challenge. And if he's wielding behind-the-scenes influence, you have the additional frustration of not knowing what channels he's using, or how he's using them.

THE CHALLENGE: It has often been observed that people in positions of great power become too removed from what's happening on the frontline. The fact that you're out there in the trenches—and the Mogul *isn't*—is probably your greatest competitive advantage. The owner of a small business who's ringing up actual sales on the cash register every day is in a better position to respond quickly to consumer trends than the Mogul who's trying to collect and interpret reports from numerous branch stores. The political candidate who's visiting communities and talking to people about what they need could be in a far better position to understand voter appeal than the politician who's gathering information from a host of media advisors.

If you're on the frontlines, if you keep your eyes and ears open, and if you trust your own judgment, you will probably have access to *information* that the Mogul doesn't have yet— and sometimes that hard information is more powerful than money or influence.

But when you're going up against a Mogul, you must also develop some of the *skills* of a Mogul. You should be able to find ways to wield your own influence and build your own network of contacts who can help you. In time, you may be able to gather the technical, financial, and human resources to challenge this person at his own level.

THE YOUNG TURK

The longer you compete and the more you improve your performance, the more confident you are likely to become. It's all the more unsettling, then, when the young turk comes along to shake you from your position.

The young turk has several alarming advantages: (1) He's been able to watch your performance and learn from it. (If he has studied carefully, he's discovered your tactics and may be able to anticipate your next move.) (2) He's up-to-date on the latest developments. The young turk, who is fresh out of school and has just learned the latest technology, may know a few things that you haven't even heard about yet. (3) He doesn't have a track record that clues you in to *his* moves. As a result, you don't know whether he's better than he looks or worse than he looks—and you don't know what he'll do next.

THE CHALLENGE: You have to take it for granted that the young turk has more youthful energy and probably more recklessness than you do. After all, he has everything to gain by knocking you from your pedestal—and nothing to lose if he fails (he'll just come back again). On the other hand, he probably hasn't had time to build a team, develop experience, and learn follow through.

The challenge is to learn his style quickly and use your greater experience to respond to the challenge. If you're in a technological field where he knows the new technology and you don't, you may need to get some self-education—fast! But that's also a benefit for you, because you have to stay up-to-date if you're going to stay sharp and competitive.

Another thing about the young turk: if he's the best of your challengers, then you want him on your team. Plant that idea in *his* mind as soon as you can.

THE HARASSER

There are competitors who just won't let go. You may win the first round against them, and they come back. You win another round, and they're back again. They try a different angle. They look for holes in your defense. They won't give up.

It's hard to feel good about the harasser. He seems to dog your footsteps and he seems intent on slowing you down. On the other hand, this is the competitor who forces you to be thorough, to look behind as well as ahead of yourself, and to plug up any holes in your defense.

If you are a salesperson and you think you have a "lock" on a particular account, your harasser is the rival who tries to move in any time you have a problem with that account. If you are an administrator, the harasser will take advantage of any slip-ups to get the attention of management and prove that he can do a better job. If he's a rival for achievement, he'll try to get the awards that you haven't gotten yet; be published where you aren't; or get funding that you don't have access to.

The harasser's harassment may even be unintentional. Most competitive people, I am sure, have some secret competition with rivals who are near and far—and each time that rival scores a success, it's as if that secret competitor has just harassed us again with his success. We just don't like to see those guys score points on us.

THE CHALLENGE: Because the harasser makes you alert to the slightest weakness in your defense, he challenges you to improve your performance every day. If you're a sportsperson who is indifferent in preparation but an outstanding competitor, the harasser forces you to practice harder. If you're a businessperson who is an outstanding marketer but an indifferent administrator, the harasser forces you to get an office manager. If you're a team leader who is poor at details, the harasser forces you to get yourself a person who is good at handling the details. You learn that if you have an area of weakness, the harasser is going to challenge you in that area.

But there's a lesson to be learned from the harasser's dogged persistence. Do *you* know the areas where your rivals are weakest? Do you keep up the pressure, so they don't get away with slipshod work? Do you always come back to challenge them? If *you* become a harasser, you also become a good competitor, because you're always looking for ways to play harder and smarter against the other guy.

To me, these types of competitors are by far the toughest to beat. No matter what you're doing—sports, business, entertainment, education, or public service—you're likely to be challenged in numerous ways, from many sides. But each type of challenge is both an education and a test of your own performance. If you can meet the challenge and beat the competitor at his strategy, you steadily increase your mastery of the game.

You Need the Opponent

Each of the competitors I have met in my own career and described above poses a legitimate competitive challenge. But they do more than that, as well. A competitor *defines the level of competition.*

Martina Navratilova made an excellent observation about this in the late seventies after she had been playing on the women's professional tennis circuit. As a leading contender, Navratilova traveled with Olga Morzova, Chris Evert, Betty Stove, Jeanie Brinkman, Jerry Diamond, and Frankie Durr. They were friends and traveling companions, but they were also intensely competitive.

After the tour, Navratilova observed:

> Being on the court with an opponent is a strange business. You're totally out for yourself, to win a match, yet you're dependent on your opponent to some degree for the type of match it is and how well you play. You need the opponent; without her you do not exist.

Although Navratilova was speaking only of tennis, her observation applies to almost any competitive activity. *You need the opponent.* You and your opponent are, in a way, involved in a collaboration because together you define the level of play—not only how *well* you're going to play, but how fairly, according to what rules of conduct, and by what measure of performance.

Ideally, we would select top-level competitors who always play fair and square, and never break the rules. It would be great if we could all show grace under pressure and prove that we could lose honorably. That isn't always the case, of course, but you and your opponent *do* decide what the rules are going to be. If two opposing teams collude in letting the game degenerate into a fistfight, then that's what the fans will see—a fistfight. If two business rivals decide that they're both going to use payoffs—then open business competition degenerates into a payoff game. But if you and your competitor are playing the same game by the same rules, just be glad he's tough to beat.

Are You Your Own Competitor?

Probably.

And probably the toughest one to beat.

Inside every competitive person, I am sure, is the mentor, the energizer, the Mogul, the young turk, and the harasser. Each of us is teaching, working, driving, wheeling and dealing, and testing ourselves all the time. We're trying to get our game together and we're always attempting to better our last performance.

In fact, competing with *yourself* may turn out to be the most difficult part of the competitive game. When something *inside* says you have to finish just one more job today; when you realize that you have to go back to the drawing board with a plan because *you're* not satisfied with it; when you suddenly realize that you have to become more enthusiastic, energetic, or clever than you've been in the past; when you remind yourself that there are calls you have to make and people you have to meet; when some inner voice tells you to be dogged and persistent and to see it through—that's the competitor in *you*, making new demands, telling you what to do.

Do you like it?

Not always. Those demands can be high. They can shake you up and wear you out. There are probably some stretches where you wish you could turn off the inner competitiveness and drop out of the race.

But if you like the competitive game, you'll keep playing. Because *you're* as tough to beat as *they* are.

PART 5

Goals

19

Do What You Love— Love What You Do

Attitude, performance, teamwork, and competition—these are the raw materials that go into the art of winning. But they are only raw materials. The only person who can put these materials together and shape them into a win for yourself is *you.*

How do you do that?

I believe you have to make *your goals* central to everything you do—so *everything else* shapes itself around them.

Your goals may start out as a secret, or they may be publicly announced from the very beginning. But whether you hold them close, or banner them from the rooftop, you have to keep affirming, constantly, every day, in large ways and small, that *you know the direction you're headed.*

Once your direction becomes clear to you and fully visible to others, all the elements of winning—attitude, performance, teamwork, and competition—begin to come together. You develop your own formula that works for you. You become so committed to your goals that, finally, you become committed to the commitment itself.

So this part of the book is really the most personal. All the other techniques of winning you can acquire through experience or

175

practice with a team—but the *goals* you set for yourself will remain uniquely yours. If I can help you to think about those goals, write them down, formulate them in your head, and begin the work—then this part of the book could perform magic for you. It can help you realize your potential!

Find the Magnetic Force

When I was a kid, I used to hang around the docks of the San Diego Yacht Club, looking for a chance to sail with anyone who would take me on as crew. That's where I began. I didn't have a boat of my own. I didn't have a rich uncle who was a world-class sailor. There was no all-star coach, standing on the sidelines, about to mutter, "Wow, that kid's got talent."

All I knew was: *I wanted to race sailboats.*

And I mean *race.* I knew from the beginning that sailing-for-the-pure-pleasure-of-sailing wasn't what I wanted. It didn't give me a thrill to tack aimlessly back and forth across the harbor. I wasn't lured by the prospect of long-distance ocean sailing: crossing the Pacific in an open boat, for example, held no spell for me. Nor was I enraptured by the size and beauty of great sailing yachts: I wasn't in it for the polished teak and fitted brass.

It was the *combination* of racing and sailing. I liked dealing with the eccentricities of wind, current, and weather, and I liked matching my wits, skill, and stamina against other sailors. Taken together, that *combination* exercised the strongest magnetic pull in my life.

There were a lot of things, in those days, that *weren't* pulling me. School. Math books. History books. Homework. I wasn't so great at following rules, doing the right thing, and staying out of trouble. But despite all the things I couldn't do and didn't like to do, *I knew could race sailboats.* That was the magnet. It had a stronger force than anything else. So when I went after my goals, I just let the magnet pull me.

Let the Magnet Do the Pulling

Chuck Yeager loves to fly planes.
Donald Trump loves to do deals.
Mario Andretti loves to race cars.
Mike Dingman loves to run companies.

What if U.S. Supreme Court Justice Sandra Day O'Connor or Chuck Yeager had gotten stuck in the real estate business? What if someone had forced Donald Trump to become a test pilot? What if Mario Andretti had to manage tens of thousands of employees? What if Mike Dingman or *Cosmopolitan* magazine's Helen Gurley Brown had to drive race cars every day?

There's a pull. A magnet. You have to recognize it and see where it's drawing you. Then you make your choices. Sometimes you have to look around at all the alternatives, figure out which course seems like the best, and commit yourself to it. In other cases, you almost can't help yourself! The pull is so strong, you don't really *have* a choice. You just give in to the pull.

Love Flying?

How much does Chuck Yeager love to fly?

On March 5, 1944, when he was twenty-one years old, Yeager bailed out of a burning P-51 above occupied France. Alone and wounded in enemy territory, Yeager hooked up with French resistance fighters who helped him reach the foothills of the Pyrenees. With one companion (a navigator from a downed B-24), risking frozen death in the icebound mountains, Yeager and the navigator hiked into the Pyrenees. A German patrol caught up with the two airmen, opened fire, and the navigator was wounded. Single-handedly, Yeager dragged his unconscious companion over the top of the Pyrenees into Spain, dragged him down the mountain to a deserted road, then walked twenty miles south to the nearest town. When he turned himself in to the local police, he was thrown into jail. He sawed through the window bars, escaped to the nearest pension, ate two helpings of chicken and beans, soaked for an hour in a hot tub, and crawled into bed and slept for two days. That's where an American consul found him.

Weeks later, back in England, he was told he was going to be sent home, which was Army Air Corps policy for pilots who had been shot down in enemy territory. Chuck refused to go. He had come to fly airplanes—and that was what he was going to do.

"Without realizing it," he later recalled, "I was about to *take charge of my life*. If I had submitted to being sent home, I doubt whether the Army Air Corps would have been interested in retaining my services when the war ended. I would probably have been mustered out and my flying career abruptly ended."

Yeager got an interview with General Eisenhower, convinced the general to let him stay, and a few days later he was flying again.

Forty-four years later, I asked Chuck what advice he would give to someone who wanted to be successful in a career—any career.

"I'd tell you to pick something you enjoy doing. Forget the money angle, within reason. If you enjoy what you're doing, you'll adjust your lifestyle to meet your income. And if you enjoy it well enough, you'll be outstanding because you'll always *like* doing it."

Love Real Estate?

Talk to anyone who has won big, and you will probably get the same story: they *like* what they're doing. Since they like it, they want to do more of it. Doing more, they get better. The better they are, the more they excel. So there's a direct connection from liking what you're doing to excelling at what you're doing.

Robert "Scott" Scott and Barbara Scott, my friends and associates in the real estate business, are people who love what they do. Barbara relishes almost all aspects of office management, from doing financial reports to letter-writing, organizing, filing, meeting with clients, and checking up on details. Scott likes to plan, make deals, take care of property, and nurture its growth.

The real estate business is a magnet for both of them. After Scott was graduated from San Diego State, with a B.A. in pre-law, he continued to work on his Masters in Business Administration. He and Barbara sought jobs in the San Diego area. Barbara became personnel secretary at First National Bank, and Scott got a job at San Diego Federal Savings & Loan.

Scott had no idea he would like the real estate business, but the more he saw of it—from the perspective of loans and appraisals— the more interested he got. After five years, he had an opportunity to work for Corky McMillin, doing land planning, housing design, and sales for Corky McMillin Development Company in San Diego County. Scott loved the real estate work, and Barbara saw an opportunity to do all the kinds of things she liked to do—the organizing, the details, the paperwork—and with Scott, they were the perfect partners for a real estate office. They opened a small office in Bonita and they've had their own business ever since.

What does Scott love about it?

"I work for myself, that's first.

"The risk-reward relationship is terrific.

"And I get to see things from start to finish—whether it's the sale of a house to someone who is really pleased, or the development of a vacant parcel of land."

They work long, hard, and intensely. Whenever they start out on a new project, there's a high risk with a big up-front investment, and it's not always clear which way a development is going. But they love the whole process—sorting out the alternatives, deciding on a plan, working toward their goal.

The financial rewards *protect* a lifestyle they're happy with.

"Some of the most rewarding moments don't come from the money," says Scott. "They come when we drive down a street where we've done something that we're proud of. We've seen it happen from start to finish—we've done something good—and that's very satisfying."

Love Politics?

After Robert Strauss left the chairmanship of the National Democratic Committee, he became Special Trade Representative in President Carter's cabinet. He concluded the Tokyo Round of

Multilateral Trade Negotiations and helped usher the Trade Act of 1979 through Congress. He was later Carter's personal representative to the Middle East Peace negotiations and, in 1981, was awarded the Presidential Medal of Freedom.

Behind the scenes in Washington, especially within the Democratic party, Strauss, at age sixty-nine, is a consummate negotiator and power broker. From his secure post in the Washington branch of the law firm he founded, Strauss is in a strategic position to wield influence with a wide array of politicians, visiting dignitaries, and journalists.

Robert Strauss has a hectic schedule that includes numerous speaking engagements, long plane flights, late-night negotiations, two-hour telephone calls, and an endless round of dinners and social occasions.

And he loves his job.

"When I get up in the morning, my wife asks me how I am this morning and I say, 'Terrific.' I say that no matter how I feel when I start out. I go into the office and by ten o'clock I've said that to two or three people. And by then I *do* feel terrific.

"I have a little sign on my desk," says Strauss, "that says, 'It *can* be done.' That's what I say, and it's what I believe. It's the reason I feel forty-six even though I'm sixty-nine."

Washington observers keep wondering what Robert Strauss really wants. More money? More prestige? More power? The presidency?

I think Robert Strauss probably wants exactly what he's got. Power, prestige, and presidential aspirations may be part of the package, but meanwhile, he loves what he does every day.

Find Your Winning Combination

Discovering exactly what you want to do may take some flexibility. Often the right combination emerges from a feeling that you're *almost* in the right place—but not quite. Or that you could *almost* love what you're doing—if you could just make a few adjustments in your schedule or your professional life. Once you've identified what's causing you the discomfort, you may have to search and explore to work out the winning combination.

Chuck Yeager knew he loved to fly—but how could he know that he would make a *career* of test-piloting new aircraft? He couldn't look into the future of jet-fighter aviation and see that he would someday be the first person to break the sound barrier. All he knew was that he would *never* be content flying passenger airplanes. He could never be comfortable with a military existence that was all paperwork and routine. Whenever there was a choice between the routine assignment or the new challenge, Chuck grabbed the challenge—until, eventually, he had the winning combination.

My friend Scott didn't wake up one morning to find out that he really wanted to sell real estate. But he could see that he didn't want to go to law school and he didn't want to stay in banking. He was fortunate to be in a banking position that put him in touch with what he really liked doing—and he just kept moving that way until he had worked out a winning combination in the real-estate business.

Robert Strauss could move back to Texas, turn his back on the long hours, the hectic schedules, the speeches, the dinners, and the long plane flights. At this point he could retire comfortably. But Washington power, the ever-changing political scene, the ability to win the respect of big policymakers—and to influence events that have national and international importance—comprises the winning combination of legal, political, social, and public life that works perfectly for Bob Strauss.

I would never have been completely comfortable in the drapery business—my combination had to include competitive sailing.

Mario Andretti would never have been comfortable racing stock cars for the rest of his life—Formula racing gave him the winning combination.

Mike Dingman started on Wall Street—but people management along with financial management turned out to be the best combination for him.

Donald Trump's family was in the apartment rental business

but he had to do bigger deals and raise taller buildings before he had the winning combination.

For each person, the combination must be different:

• For a big-company lawyer who no longer finds the work stimulating, a winning combination could mean working for a smaller company and getting involved in management as well as legal work.

• For the manager who wants to be less of a generalist and more of a specialist, the winning combination might be intense concentration on one area of technology, business, managerial development, or financial growth.

• For someone who feels underemployed and understimulated in their day-to-day work, the winning combination might be part-time employment, allowing more free time to pursue some strong interests.

And of course the combination changes during your lifetime. Certain interests begin to outweigh others, and you mature in your ability to manage people, conduct business, or play the game you're best at. As opportunities arise, new goals come within reach that you never could have imagined before. Naturally, you seek new challenges. But each time there is a change in your position, or a new win, you start working again toward putting together the winning *combination*—that is, the particular combination that works for *you*.

Give It a Chance

If you put a lead shield around a magnet, the attraction stops. There's no pull at all.

If someone had successfully kept me away from sailboats, I don't know what would have happened. I suppose all my desire to win would have gone into some other enterprise, and maybe I would have been successful in competing and winning at something else. But I'm glad no one *did* stop me. I was lucky to grow up in a great place for competitive sailing, and I was lucky to meet top sailors when I was still young. But above all, I was lucky that nothing *prevented* me from sailing competitively.

If you want the magnetic force to go to work, you have to give it a chance. Here are some ways to do that:

1. GIVE YOURSELF ROOM TO MANEUVER

Many people divide their activities into two basic categories— things we *have* to do and things we *like* to do. If you have a lot of outside commitments that don't seem very meaningful or important, you just have to maneuver around them until you get to the things you *like* to do. Not once or twice a week, or once a month. Not just during vacation or on weekends. But *as often as possible!*

When you're setting your goals, look at things that give you the greatest satisfaction—the biggest sense of accomplishment. Is it some aspect of your work or profession? Is it an association with one group of people? A particular skill? A sport? A hobby?

Skip the money angle for a minute. Never mind whether other people place any value on what attracts you. Just look hard at the thing that really rewards you, even if it isn't important to your boss, your spouse, your best friend, your financial advisor, or your neighbor.

Once you've identified that, you have to maneuver so you have time and energy for whatever it is that you want to pursue. Maybe it's "just" a hobby:

• Do you love to build model airplanes? Go fly them once a week. Join the model airplane club. Make time to work on model airplanes before you go to work in the morning and after you get home from work at night. Go to rallies. Perhaps one day you'll decide to set up a shop for yourself.

• Do you get a charge out of woodworking in your basement? Experiment with different projects. Try to sell your handiwork at crafts fairs or perhaps through coupon ads in woodworking magazines.

• Do you like to play around on the computer? Develop some programs of your own. Get that software you're curious about and test it out; ask yourself whether you could do a better job.

• Is playing the saxophone your thing? Find a teacher. Begin practicing. Jam with a group. Try out for a performance.

You may find that one part of your current job holds an oversize attraction. Identify it:

• Making a client happy—with great on-time performance, wonderful service, or a product that's just right.
• Producing a well-written report that has a real impact on company policy.
• Launching a crash program to meet a deadline before your competitor beats you.
• Motivating people to learn, work together, develop their skills, and get a job done.

If you *let the magnet pull you,* who knows where it can lead? People who love to play around with model airplanes can end up with careers in aviation. The guy who gets a kick out of making beer in his basement might start a highly successful microbrewery. Someone who enjoys computer programming ends up creating a new piece of software that beats anything on the market. The amateur saxophone player leaves his nine-to-five job and makes a career for himself in the music business.

If you like working with clients better than anything else about your job, why not steer yourself toward sales? If you like report writing, you may be headed toward a future as an independent consultant. If you're the person who likes to work on crash programs and meet deadlines, find a position where the pressure is on you. If you're someone who wants to motivate and lead people, you'll never be satisfied until you have management responsibilities.

You might as well start maneuvering toward something you

love—making room for it, fitting it in, and finding the time—
because *you have to give it a chance.*

2. GO WITH IT

Once you let the magnet go to work, and you start seeing which
way it's pulling you, you still have a choice. You can drop the lead
shield between you and the magnet and say to yourself, "That's
enough—no more model airplanes (or brewed beer, or computer
programs, or saxophone playing)!" You can back off from making
a change ("I can't go looking for another job right now." "I
should be happy I'm employed.") You can command yourself to
get back to "serious" work. Or you can go with the magnetic force
and see where it takes you.

In my own case, I let sailboat racing pull me as hard as it
wanted to. Once I started competing, I wanted to compete more
and more. For the vast majority of sailors in the world, racing is
not a profession. For most sailors, it falls somewhere between the
category of a sport and a hobby.

So I had to decide. Should I go ahead with something that
never really promised to support me and my family, put my kids
through school, and pay the mortgage? Everyone who jumps feet
first into a new enterprise or makes a bigger commitment to
something is likely to face this kind of dilemma. Often there's a
high risk with no guarantee of a payoff.

But if you pursue what you love to do, and you keep at it long
enough, you'll often find people who are willing to support your
efforts. They may not give you direct financial support, but if you
believe strongly in what you're doing, and you show real commitment, they'll help you find ways to make it through and achieve
your goals.

3. FIND THE CENTRAL MAGNET

But what if you're pulled in too many directions? What if there's
too much you like to do?

This is when it's important to *find the central magnet.* You may have to list your priorities on a sheet of paper, study them, and figure out *which ones are most important.* There are *real choices* to be made. Are you really being pulled in different directions—or are you *letting* yourself be pulled because you're afraid of commitment? Are you afraid of losing? Would you rather not take certain risks?

Everyone has some goals in his lifetime. Sometimes hundreds of goals, ranging from the monumental to the minuscule. Many of them will be reachable, but you have to put them in order. If you are pulled in many directions, you just have to work that much harder to achieve the winning combination. Find the central magnet—put that first on your list—and let it pull you. Have confidence that everything else will fall into line.

4. TAKE THE PLUNGE

When that magnetic pull is at full force, you will probably reach the point where you have to take the plunge.

In my case, I couldn't get enough of sailboat racing. I was always looking ahead toward the next race, the next level of competition, a new class of boat (new challenges)! And I found out that *when you can't get enough of it,* you may have some hard choices to make. How can you *afford* to do what you love? Can you get your family and friends to tolerate the commitment that you want to make toward your goals. Do they understand why you keep doing what you want to do?

Every race I entered pulled me away from my business and my family. When I started traveling east for the SORC races and traveling overseas for international competition, I was sometimes gone for weeks. When I got into America's Cup competition, the drain on my personal resources was enormous—once again, my friends, family, and business partners had to put up with someone who was almost totally preoccupied with something other than friendships, family affairs, and business dealings.

At some point, you have to decide whether to go ahead. That

powerful magnet begins to change everything you do. It changes your attitude—because you're doing what you love. It changes your performance—because you always want to do more. It improves teamwork—because your energy and enthusiasm brings people into your camp and motivates them to achieve new heights of accomplishment. It raises the level of competition—because you're working so hard to win that you're always striving to get better. And once the magnet hits the steel, nothing can pry them apart.

20

What's Within Reach?

Sometimes, the first goals that we set for ourselves are so high and ambitious that they may be completely unrealistic or unattainable. Experience teaches us lessons, of course, and we revise our goals accordingly. But there is always a trade-off between setting goals that are so high that they are beyond reach on the one hand—and, on the other hand, setting goals that are so easy to reach that we aren't forced to stretch farther, work harder, and use all our potential powers.

When you're setting goals for yourself, I think you have to regard goal-setting as a *process* rather than a formula. In the early part of that process, find goals that are achievable. Achievability can be measured in a number of ways—by the standards of your own performance, in terms of what other people of similar abilities have done in the past, and in terms of what is realistically possible at this stage of your life, your career, or your development. Once you have set that achievable goal, *then* you try to reach it—and that's when attitude, performance, teamwork, and competition all come into play.

Afterward, there is a process of setting new goals or revising previous goals. This process of meeting one goal and determining the next never stops. You have to constantly look at where you are now, then figure out what you can accomplish in a given amount of time. I don't know whether this process ever becomes automatic. You have to keep working it out. Is the goal important enough? Are the challenges real? Is the "win" something that you really want?

But the process of setting goals *can* improve with practice. With practice, you gain greater appreciation for the highs and lows of your own performance; with practice, you begin to see what you *can* achieve; with practice, you find out which challenges outweigh the importance of others. Reaching a personal goal—whether or not anyone else knows about it—carries its own reward. When you get good at the whole *process* of setting goals and meeting them, you get good at the art of winning.

THE PROCESS—PART 1
TEST FOR REACHABILITY

Eugene Lang, the son of a Hungarian-born machinist, grew up in an East Harlem tenement. When he was eight he started his first business, making and selling wooden checkers. At fourteen he graduated from high school and took a dishwashing job in a restaurant.

One night when he was filling in for a waiter, a customer asked Eugene Lang why he wasn't in school. Eugene said he'd already graduated, but he would go on to college if he had the opportunity. The customer turned out to be a trustee of Swarthmore College. He set up a meeting between Lang and a dean at Swarthmore—a meeting which resulted in Lang receiving a full scholarship.

From Swarthmore Lang went on to get his MBA from Columbia. During the war, he set up a shop in his garage and began manufacturing his own invention—the heli-coil, a fastening system for airplane and car parts. As the company continued to grow, Lang started a factory, began exporting the heli-coil, and created the REFAC Technology Development Corporation.

On June 25, 1981, Eugene Lang, now a multimillionaire, gave an inspirational graduation speech at the Harlem elementary school where he had graduated fifty-three years earlier. Addressing the sixty-one sixth graders in caps and gowns who filled the front rows of the auditorium, he started off saying things like, "Dream of what you want to be, the kind of life you wish to build. And believe in that dream. Be prepared to work for it. . . ."

But as his speech continued, Lang realized that the dream he was talking about was completely unreachable for most of these kids. They lived in poverty. They were surrounded by drugs and crime. Ninety percent of them were destined to drop out before finishing high school. The dream he was eulogizing had nothing to do with reality.

And that's when Eugene Lang made the promise which has hit the press like the shot heard round the world: "Stay in school," he said, "and I will give each of you a *college scholarship!*"

Six years later, one student had dropped out and one ended up behind bars. But fifty-nine stuck with it—in a neighborhood where, normally, only five kids from that class would have made it through high school.

Eugene Lang did more than offer a goal. He made it *reachable*—just as a Swarthmore trustee had made a college education reachable for Eugene Lang, decades before.

When you're setting goals—especially short-term goals—you have to take the reachability factors into account. Grandiose schemes are wonderful, but if they're based on illusions about how much you can accomplish or how far you can reach, they could evaporate into the mists of inspiration and never be seen again. Take the short steps first—and check out the precedents:

· *What did other people do?* Be insatiably curious about all those people who headed the direction you're going—and made it. Ask them, ask their friends, ask anyone who knows about them what steps they took. Read interviews, biographies, "insider" books. Trace the tracks of your hero—find out how that hero achieved his goals.

• *Pay attention to the steps.* And when you're tracing those steps, note the details. What schools did that person attend or how was he trained? Who influenced him? How did he learn, practice, or study before striking out on his own? Your own plans will have to include details—not just vague, general aspirations—if you are going to reach *real* goals.

• *How long did it take that person?* When you're considering how another person reached her goals, pay special attention to the time frame. Is it likely to take months—or years—to get as far as she went?

• *Can you do better?* Having looked at the steps and the time frame, you're in a position to measure your abilities and resources against your hero's. Is there anything you can do better or faster? Do you have a head start in some respects? If so, you might be able to set *more* ambitious goals than he did.

THE PROCESS—PART 2
SET A TIME LIMIT

For anyone in sports, working *toward* a goal means working *against* a time limit. You only have so long until the beginning of the season, the next game, the next race. No matter what else is going on in your life, the deadline is always creeping up on you.

In business you face the pressure of other kinds of deadlines—deadlines for meeting quotas, preparing proposals, reporting results, solving problems, launching new products, staging events.

But for each of us, many of the real time limits are personal: they're self-imposed.

You can get your degree in four years—or twenty-four.

You can send out your résumé next month—or next year.

The phone call that *might* bring you closer to your goal can always wait until tomorrow.

The letter that *could* be written this morning can be put off until this afternoon.

But the people who come closest to achieving their goals *set their own time limits.* And then work like hell to meet them.

Alex Spanos, president and chairman of the board of the San Diego Chargers, is the son of Greek immigrants. He grew up in Stockton, California, and graduated from the University of Pacific, where he earned letters in swimming and diving. Alex went into the construction business, and in 1960 he formed the A. G. Spanos Construction company, which has built more than 55,000 apartment units across the U.S., representing 2.7 million square feet of commercial property. A great civic booster in San Diego, he supports drives for the Children's Hospital and Health Center, the County Easter Seals Telethon, and the annual United Way/CHAD drives. He keeps up his amateur golf, too; Alex won the Bob Hope Desert Pro-Am Classic at Palm Desert in 1977 and the British Amateur Golf Championship in 1980.

"Throughout my life," says Spanos, "I have always set five-year goals for what I wanted to accomplish. And I have achieved each of those goals in *less* than five years."

Spanos's five-year limit was arbitrary. He could have made it three, four, six, or seven. But once he started thinking in terms of five-year plans for himself and his company, he began to structure his goals around those five-year intervals. And he automatically renewed his commitment to *new* goals every five years.

What is *your* time frame? If there are no outside deadlines set by other people, you might put yourself on a quarterly plan, a yearly plan, or a four-year plan for meeting your goals. Once you get into the habit of measuring progress in time-spans, that interval becomes an opportunity to check in with yourself, see how far you've come, and look ahead to where the next goals lie.

Here's what the *process* of setting up a time frame looks like:

• *Set the time limit.* What's the *minimum* time it could take you to reach your goal? Once you've identified that minimum, you have to decide whether that's a feasible time frame for *you.* Consider whether this goal represents something new for you—

and therefore something that will take longer than you expect. Make the time frame reasonable, but demanding.

· *Break it down.* Once you have the whole frame—say, one year—then analyze what must be done within each time segment (each month, for instance) to achieve your goal. It's like putting up a building; after you have the blueprint, figure out in which order the deliveries should be made and when each phase of construction work should be done.

· *Announce the schedule.* If you're working closely with a team, of course they should be the first to know the schedule. But other people, as well, need to be informed—including friends, family, and business associates. That way, they'll *know* what phase of the schedule you're in.

· Once you have the time limit, you've broken it down, and you've announced the schedule, *decide what you're going to do today to get started.* This tops off all the goal-setting you've started to do. If you now have a clear goal and a schedule, start the clock running *now.*

THE PROCESS—PART 3
MAKE YOUR GOALS VISIBLE

In every kind of education, sport, business, or enterprise, there are some visible signs of success—indications that you have begun to reach some of your goals. In education, of course, it's the diploma. In sports, the ribbons and trophies. In business, the title on the door. In a new enterprise, it's that first dollar you take in, or the new expansion, or your first big celebration. Each of these visible signs of success is a reward for the progress you're making toward reaching your goals.

And those *visible* rewards are important. They assure you that you are *on your way:* you *are* reaching your goals.

There are at least three ways to make your goals more visible:

1. Building blocks. Let's say you post the schedule for your team. That's your visible building block. Every day the guys glance at the schedule as they come in the door. They know where they stand and they see the date by which it all has to come together. Every date on that calendar is a visible building block.

There are also building blocks of the image-making kind. If you print up a card that announces your new enterprise, you make that enterprise *visible*. People can hold your card, get an image of your company, and be assured that you're actually in business. Victor Kiam, the man who bought Remington Shavers, started out his business life in Paris after the war with a used Simca sedan and a pack of business cards advertising the "European Touring Service, Incorporated." The cards were only symbolic, of course—he had no corporation, as such. But those cards became *building blocks* toward his goal—to build a profitable touring business. (Two years later, after paying off the expenses and pocketing the profit, Kiam headed home to Harvard Business School.)

Whether your building block is a gilt title on the door (position), a diploma on the wall (education), or a date on the calendar (deadline), you're making your progress visible.

2. Milestones. The milestones also show your progress. They're the badges, ribbons, and honors that are awarded to successful people and successful *teams* of people. A new production figure marked on the floor of a factory can also be a milestone. Post the first dollar made as the *first* milestone; later on, post the millionth dollar as *another* milestone. (Remember McDonald's amazingly effective advertising campaign? "Over _____ million sold!" was posted on all its signs. McDonald's got every hamburger buyer in America to become a part of its new-milestone campaign.)

3. Bonanzas. If you have reached your goals of success, wealth, or preeminence, why not enjoy the rewards of achievement? Treat yourself to whatever symbols of success make you feel the hard work has been worth the effort. Perhaps a vacation is in order, or that car you've always wanted to own. You can make your success visible with reminders, such as pictures in your office, or furnishings that reflect your taste and your success. Anything that reminds you that you have achieved the big goals that you set for yourself is worthy of display.

You're the Goalkeeper

If you stop setting goals for yourself, it's highly unlikely that anyone will ask you to start again.

If your goals are always so high that they're unreachable, few people would remind you that you're being too starry-eyed.

If your goals aren't big enough, probably only a few people can persuade you to reach higher.

For all these reasons, you are the caretaker of your own goals. Others can lend advice. They might provide you with fresh insights or information. But they can't help you set your goals or convince you to pursue them. That's a commitment you have to make for yourself.

21

Commitment to
the Commitment

When I began this book, America's Cup XXVII was still many months ahead, and I had no idea what the outcome would be. In fact, the way things were going in the courts, I wasn't even sure whether the race would be sailed.

But now the 1988 America's Cup is history. Our sixty-foot catamaran with the wing sail defended the Cup by beating the gigantic Kiwi "K-boat" in two consecutive races. In the first race, *Stars & Stripes* led *KZ-1* around the course to win by 18 minutes, 15 seconds; in the second, we won by 21 minutes, 8 seconds.

Today, the *Stars & Stripes '88* and *KZ-1* compounds in San Diego Harbor have closed down. The crews have gone their separate ways, for now.

Though we won the race on the water, we knew we might not have seen the last of Michael Fay. We had to wait and see what his next move would be.

In 1987 I'd begun to respond to Fay's unorthodox challenge by relying on the key principles that have served me for as long as I can remember: attitude, performance, teamwork, competition, and goals. Now, with the advantage of hindsight, I have an opportunity to reflect on how those five elements came together for

America's Cup XXVII, the contest in San Diego that came to a head on September 7 and 9, 1988.

As usual, the race that took place on the water represented only a small percentage of the before-the-race and behind-the-scenes battle to win the Cup. And the fact that *Stars & Stripes '88* won both races in the best-of-three series by minutes rather than seconds does not mean that it was an easy match. On the contrary, in many respects it was the toughest I have ever raced, because so much of the competition took place in the courts, in the committee rooms, and at press conferences instead of on the water. But for that very reason, it's interesting to look at what *did* happen—and how the elements came together to produce a win for *Stars & Stripes '88.*

Attitude

How could anyone have a great *attitude* about a challenge like Michael Fay's?

To me it was a sneak attack, another Pearl Harbor. When he challenged the San Diego Yacht Club with a 132-foot monohull in the summer of 1987, he knew there was no other boat like it in the world. To me the reason that Fay chose to challenge with a monohull was transparent; his purpose was to make sure he won the design contest before the race began, so that no U.S. syndicate could mount a serious defense, and no other challenger would have a chance to prepare for the race. As I saw it, Michael Fay envisioned an easy race against a poorly prepared defender.

The problem was—as a competitive sailor who relishes a great match race—how could I take the challenge seriously? I literally did not want to believe it was happening. How could we fight so hard to win the Cup in '87, only to have a challenger rip it from our hands because a hundred-year-old Deed of Gift left a legal loophole? It didn't seem right, it didn't seem fair, and I didn't think they'd get away with it.

But after the New Zealanders had their day in court and the

judge said it *was* right and fair, I had to face the awful prospect that they might also get away with it.

That's when my attitude changed. It had to. We had to *make a commitment* to holding on to the America's Cup, using all the resources at our command. And once we were committed to the campaign, we had to go all-out on every front—hire better lawyers, raise more money, build a faster boat, even conduct a tougher PR campaign than Michael Fay, which was difficult considering the fact that his main business is merchant banking. We'd do whatever it took to hold on to the Cup that we'd won in a fair contest less than a year before.

That attitude-change didn't come overnight, but when it came—when I made the commitment in my own mind—we immediately started to prepare for a race that was just a few months away. Suddenly I was looking at a campaign where everything was speeded up, with hundreds of unknown factors to consider. Could we come up with a design that would beat the Kiwis in the usually light winds off San Diego? Would we be forced to defend our catamaran design in the courts? Did we have enough time to build a boat and rig that wouldn't break down and get the on-board practice we needed to win? If we *did* produce an unbeatable boat for the defense, would the New Zealanders show up for the race? Would other challengers be allowed to enter the competition?

All these questions could be answered, the problems could be solved, the boat could be built—but before anything happened, I had to go into this Cup with the attitude that we were *going* to win, and with the commitment to make that happen.

Performance

The most critical part of performance—the *homework*—had to be done with lightning speed. I've already described the great job that our design team performed in an amazingly short time. The fact that they designed and built two sixty-foot, high-performance catamarans and had them both in the water by June 1—just six months after the challenge was deemed valid—is phenomenal. Once we had them, the team put hundreds of hours into tune-ups, dealing with the inevitable breakdowns, matching the boats against each other to see how they performed. As it turned out, the early performance of the hard wing sail catamaran required that we build a second, larger (by 40 percent) wing sail. That second boat was not ready to compete until August 1. After that, we sailed eleven match-races pitting the hard-wing sail and softsail catamarans against each other in our own defender trials prior to the America's Cup race.

Getting the boats in the water, trying them out, tuning them up, and practicing with the crews were only a few phases of the total performance. Meanwhile, we also had to prepare a *Stars & Stripes '88* compound where the boats could be taken out of the water and, in the case of the wing sail, safely stowed at night. We had to prepare a court defense for the right to race the catamaran, and we had to assemble a press office to handle the publicity. And when the Kiwis again challenged us in the courts, we had to put together an unbeatable legal defense team.

All this took capital. We couldn't do it without the backing of some loyal sponsors, but even while we were asking for their support, we had to acknowledge that a court decision was still pending—and probably would be until shortly before the race.

When our list of sponsors grew longer, so did our obligations as host to the event. Dozens of corporate leaders would be arriving in San Diego to see the race—the spectator fleet turned out to be one of the largest ever at an America's Cup race—and every one of our visitors would expect first-class treatment.

For months, all these preparations had to be undertaken against a background of uncertainty. Until Judge Carmen Ciparick of the New York Supreme Court issued her decision on July 25, 1988—stating that the races should proceed—we did not know from day to day whether we were spending millions of dollars and putting in thousands of hours of preparation for nothing. We were confident that we had a sound defense, but confidence is not the same as certainty

Nonetheless, we couldn't take a "wait and see" posture. We had to work on our performance every day, so we *would* be at our best if the race began on the appointed day.

Teamwork

The kind of teamwork that went into the '88 campaign was much different from that of the '87 campaign. Before the concluding race against *Kookaburra III* in February 1987, the *Stars & Stripes* team had spent eighteen months together in a situation that was almost like boot camp. Before the America's Cup challenger round-robins began in October 1986, we'd been off in Hawaii in our own compound. Up at five every morning for workouts, on the water all day, seeing to the equipment at night, we lived, breathed, and worked constantly toward a fixed goal. As the *Stars & Stripes* crew trained in 12-meters, the factors that never changed were the date and rules of the race.

In 1988, teamwork had a different form. Between April and September 1988, the crews were lucky to squeeze in twenty or thirty hours of practice each week. We weren't off in a compound in Hawaii—we were in San Diego, close to the office and close to home. We had to compress months of preparation into weeks, and despite round-the-clock work by the support crew, we did miss many hours on the water due to breakdowns and maintenance work.

But team-building was just as important as it had been in the previous campaign, and the people who crewed in the two races of the '88 Cup were just as carefully chosen and well prepared for what we had to do. Five veterans of the '87 campaign came back for '88. All of them were new to catamaran sailing when we started out, but by the time we raced, they were as skilled as any catamaran sailors in the world. In addition, there were new members of the team that we handpicked for their catamaran and small boat experience.

Though we didn't have the thousands of hours of on-the-water practice that we had in '87, every member of the team understood the no-excuse-to-lose principle from the very beginning. For everyone on the crew and shore team, making America's Cup '88 go the way we wanted it to was really a test of the depth of our skill and experience. And every one who joined the team was just as committed as I was to winning America's Cup XXVII.

Competition

Some tense words were uttered by Michael Fay and me, but I hope that five years from now I will finally be able to look back and say my competitor did several good things for the America's Cup. First of all, his challenge put the world on notice that there are some major flaws in the Deed of Gift. His actions pointed out that the Deed should be amended to ensure that the Cup can continue to grow and prosper as a multinational event, open to all comers on a fair basis. Secondly, by building *KZ-1* with its fifteen-story mast and enormous sail—and challenging us to build a boat that was lighter, faster, and more maneuverable—the challenge stretched modern technology of boat design and construction to its limits. And thirdly, Michael Fay reminded everyone that other boats besides 12-meters could be sailed in America's Cup competition.

When you look at the 1988 America's Cup defense as a whole, from the day Fay's unorthodox challenge arrived till the day *Stars & Stripes* crossed the line ahead of New Zealand in race 2 on September 9, 1988, Michael Fay was *very* tough to beat. Before *KZ-1* came along, we were somewhat complacently anticipating a great 12-meter race in 1991; suddenly, with his surprise attack, an aggressive competitor altered those plans.

Ultimately, the competition did what it was supposed to—it tested us to our limits. It was an unprecedented race against time to create a defender that was as technologically unusual as the challenger. For Sail America and the *Stars & Stripes '88* team that had to approach sponsors for support, it was a full-scale test of the good relations and credibility that we'd built up by always delivering what we'd promised. For the team, it was an all-out test of competitive drive: were they willing to take the gamble and put in a great effort in order to drive the challenger from our shores?

Michael Fay, as well as the designers, builders, and crew of *KZ-1* were as tough as any competitors can be. They tested us in ways that we'd never been tested before: we had to watch them all the time, and try to anticipate their every move. They reminded us, in case we needed any reminding, that the defender of the America's Cup doesn't have any special privileges.

And I can say it now: I'm glad they were tough to beat.

Goals

What *were* our goals?

In the heat of competition, it sometimes seemed as if our goals were changing every day. Unpredictability was one of the most frustrating aspects of America's Cup XXVII. At first our goal was to beat New Zealand in court, so an unnecessary race would not have to take place and we could get on with preparations for '91.

When the court accepted the terms of Michael Fay's challenge, our next goal had to be to win the design contest—to build a boat that was faster than the New Zealander's, that would not break down and would fit within the guidelines specified by the Deed of Gift.

But we had to switch goals again when Michael Fay brought us back into court over the issue of the catamaran. In another phase of this contest, our goal was to put together a legal defense team that would defend our right to race a boat that was already sailing!

And finally, when all the objections were cleared away, our goal was to sail the best race possible—with no breakdowns—and defend the Cup on the water.

Commitment to the Commitment

Through all those months of preparation accompanied by numerous frustrations, there was one steady principle that helped light the way. And America's Cup XXVII is a perfect example of how this final principle can work in your favor when all else fails.

It's what I call *the commitment to the commitment.*

When we said to Michael Fay that we accepted his challenge and we'd meet him on the water in September 1988, we made the *commitment.* No matter what else happened, I couldn't get away from that. Court decisions might go against us, rules could be debated and reinterpreted, the press could get angry, Michael Fay could try numerous tactics to change the challenge—but none of that changed our *commitment to the commitment.* What that meant was that we'd be at the starting line, ready to race, when the race began.

I believe each of us has opportunities to make a *commitment to the commitment,* no matter what goals we pursue. Though we may have lofty goals and high ambitions when we begin, what sees us through to what we *want* to accomplish are the commitments that we make along the way. Whether you write a letter accepting a challenge, or tell your manager you want to take on a difficult job; whether you sign up for school, service, or employment or you tell your spouse or best friend that you're going to go ahead with a project; whether you put your money and reputation on the line or just make a promise that you intend to keep, that *commitment to the commitment* is the vital first step toward a winning effort.

Index